CHURCH,
STATE AND
THE CONSTITUTION

CHURCH,
STATE AND
THE CONSTITUTION

George Goldberg

REGNERY GATEWAY
Washington D.C.

LIBRARY OF CONGRESS CATALOGING-IN-PUBLICATION DATA

Goldberg, George, 1935–
Church, state and the constitution.
Bibliography: p.
1. Church and state—United States—
History.   2. United States—Church history.
I. Title.
BR516.G568   1987   342.73'0852   87–4566
ISBN 0–89526–794–2 347.302852

Published in the United States by
Regnery Gateway
1130 17th Street, NW
Washington, D.C. 20036

Distributed to the trade by
Kampmann & Company, Inc.
9 E 40th Street
New York, NY 10016

10 9 8 7 6 5 4 3 2 1

Lawyers who take seriously recent U.S. Supreme Court historical scholarship as applied to the Constitution also probably believe in the Tooth Fairy and the Easter Bunny.

> *— Chief Justice Richard Neely of the West Virginia Supreme Court of Appeals*

If we wish to live off fairy tales, it may be instructive to remember that the tooth fairy demands a piece of our children before she pays up, and we have to supply the cash.

> *— Professor Loren Baritz, Provost of the U. of Massachusetts*

Table of Contents

Personal Preface

MIDWOOD HIGH SCHOOL on Bedford Avenue
in the heart of Brooklyn was about half Jewish in the Truman years. Or maybe 25 percent or 75 percent. Anyway, there were lots of Jewish kids and lots of kids who weren't Jewish. I am uncertain about the precise proportion because it really didn't matter much.

The Midwood Chorus had about the same proportion, I guess, as the overall school. Of far greater importance, it was a great chorus—Arturo Toscanini said it was the best amateur teenage chorus he ever heard. There were a hundred and fifty of us.

Very few of us were destined for musical careers. Very few of us were all that talented. Everyone could carry a tune, of course. A dozen or so had exceptional voices. A few could even read music. But for all of us, for the years we belonged to the chorus, music was our life.

We owed it all, needless to say, to the director of the chorus, George Levine, universally known as "Boss." We loved him as only a benevolent tyrant can be loved. He enriched our lives immeasurably.

Boss had been a concert pianist with a highly promising career who could not take the stress of that kind of life. He was, that is to say, first and foremost a musician, only secondarily a teacher. He had in fact little patience with the traditional curriculum of public high school music instruction. He did not teach us sight reading nor a single fact about any composer whose music we sang. I rather doubt whether he could have given you Beethoven's years or the Koechel number of *The Magic Flute* or the names of three poets set to music by Schubert. Had you asked him about such things he would doubtless have laughed at you and got on with his serious business, which was to turn a hundred and fifty sows' ears into a semblance of a silk purse.

When a new song was introduced, Boss played it through on the piano and those of us who could read were invited to sing or hum along. Then he played it through a second time with perhaps half the chorus now able to follow along. Then he put it aside and conducted us in a piece we already knew.

Next day, we learned the words, which were nearly always in English, but if not, then with a word-for-word translation. First we read them through silently and either asked about words whose meaning was unclear or confirmed that we understood every word. Then we spoke the words slowly in unison. Then we listened quietly while Boss read the words with feeling, as at a poetry reading. Then Boss had us try to mimic his reading. Again the period ended with the singing of a familiar song or two.

Next day, after five minutes of warming-up exercises for the whole chorus, Boss started with the basses, going through their entire part note by note while the other sections concentrated on how their parts seemed to coordinate with the bass part. The next three rehearsals followed the same pattern with the tenor, alto, and soprano sections. Then, the next day, Boss again played the entire piece through with the chorus singing quietly or humming along.

Then we got down to work. Now the piece was broken into phrases, the phrases into measures, and sometimes the measures into single intervals. Difficult passages were dissected into their elements and these were practiced over and over until the difficulties were fully overcome. A great deal of time was spent on cues: teaching the altos that at letter B they could get their note from the next-to-last note sung by the basses, the tenors that three measures before C they must come in on the second beat a fifth below the last note sung by the sopranos, and so forth. When the piece had been reduced to its most elementary particles, and each of those particles was as perfectly formed as possible, the task of combination began. Gradually the tempo, which had been slowed almost to stasis, was picked up. Soon the contours of the work began to appear through the mist; the excitement was palpable.

But then, just as we began to imagine we had mastered the work, Boss mixed up the sections. He had the tenors sing the alto part, the altos sing tenor, the basses and sopranos reverse roles. Quality of sound was not important now; it was permissible to sing falsetto or to omit a note beyond range, but accuracy of pitch, tempo, and dynamics was essential. The first run-through this way was invariably chaotic and funny, and it was all right to laugh—Boss himself bubbled over at some of the more amusing effects. Then he became serious again, and we were expected to follow suit without undue delay. It was time for the entire chorus to sing through each of the parts together, in unison or where necessary at the octave, while Boss stopped us at each difficult passage to explain the difficulty and perhaps suggest what other sections could do to help. Soon each of us had not only memorized his or her own part—we never performed with music—but had also nearly memorized every other part. Many members of the chorus could sing from memory every part in every piece in our repertoire.

There was still an important step to take before we had added a new song to our repertoire: we had to get into the spirit of it. If it were a ballad like "Madame Jeanette" or "Charm Me Asleep" (the translation of a German folk-song setting by Brahms) or a contemplative religious piece like "Adoramus Te," Boss would begin by creating the calmest possible atmosphere. He would stand quietly in front of the chorus, arms extended at shoulder height, hands outstretched, eyes closed in meditation. Slowly he would open his eyes and, smiling beatifically, seem to look at each of us individually, slightly nodding his head as if to acknowledge contact with a kindred spirit. Then he would softly ask us to mouth the words silently as he conducted, and, using gestures so small they could not be seen without the greatest concentration, he would lead us through this ghostly rendition. Then he would have us sing it through again, humming our parts softly. Finally, his shoulders raised in a shrug of anticipated ecstasy, his eyes shut tight, his brows contracted, he would hold his hands out in front of him with the palms facing us as if to stop us before we started, and then, his whole body quivering with the admonition to sing softly, he would begin to conduct; and as the first note sounded he would recoil as if struck by a whip, and so with the second note, and the third, until at last one hundred and fifty voices were singing together with no more sound than trees rustling in a forest or water gurgling through a brook, two Schubertian images Boss was especially fond of.

But most of our songs were lively, and they brought out Boss' talents as a dancer. He would stand in front of us, hold his arms out at shoulder length and bend them forward at the elbows while his hands dangled loosely down, and he would start to bounce on his toes. Up and down he went, up and down, and soon he had the chorus bouncing in their seats. A giggle here, a laugh there; he just kept bouncing, moving his body now from side to side, beginning to laugh himself. Suddenly he would mouth the word "Whisper!" and he would lead us through the spiritual or whatever we were learning with exaggerated rhythm but almost no sound. Then he would have us sing it full voice, then whispering a phrase, then full voice again, then clapping, stomping, another whispering chorus, then—"Stand!" — and we would sing out at the top of our voices, every muscle in our bodies keeping time to the music. Always we finished in a state of utter physical and emotional exhaustion—and exaltation.

As I said, we lived music. On weekends we met at street corners and pizza parlors; we took them over, ninety or a hundred of us. Most of the time people gathered around us to listen as we sang "Ride The Chariot" and "Didn't My Lord Deliver Daniel" and "Madame Jeanette" and "Adoramus Te" and "Hallelujah Amen" from Handel's *Judas Maccabeus.* Sometimes, though, anxious citizens called the police as they watched this huge gang of teenagers gathering on a street corner, surely up to no good.

I remember one Christmas in particular when we went carolling at old people's homes and children's hospital wards. As usual we met at the junction of Flatbush and Nostrand Avenues. It was a

perfect Christmas Eve, large flakes of snow falling quietly and set-
tling on the shoulders of our coats and on our hats as we sang.
Evidently a good citizen did call the cops, for soon a squad car
squealed up to us, light revolving like the chandelier at a school
dance. The driver stayed in the car, though; only one policeman got
out, and we thought this a good sign, for no cop looking for trouble
would tackle alone such a mob as we were.

"Are you the young troublemakers?" he asked us with a brogue
worthy of Barry FitzGerald.

We told him we were only preparing to carol.

"I thought as much," he said. "I was on the desk when the call
came in. I realized in a flash what it was and I wasn't about to miss
it. Can I join you?"

He had a lovely Irish tenor voice. Did we know the Bach-Gounod "Ave Maria?" he asked. We did indeed, and provided a humming background and a simulated harpsichord accompaniment for
him. He sang it beautifully and added a new dimension for us. We
had enjoyed singing Gounod's melody and wondering if we would
ever have thought of setting a song to the exercise-like first prelude
of Bach's *Well-Tempered Clavier.* But to our policeman it was an
expression of faith. We were moved. We also enjoyed having a
police escort for the rest of the evening.

We were therefore somewhat prepared for our next experience
with the "Ave Maria," though it came about not under a shower
of snow but on the sunlit sand of Jones Beach. It was a hot June day
and the beach on the south shore of Long Island was crowded. We
were some hundred and twenty strong that day and in good voice.
The air was still and the sound carried well, and soon we were
surrounded by one of our largest audiences ever. We sang spirituals
and a potpourri from *The Mikado*— happy, lively music, appropriate to the occasion. At a momentary lull, a nun came towards us
with a small boy in tow. She was all dressed in black and white—
nuns had not yet taken to designer habits—and made an almost
frightening image on the sun-whitened beach. As I was conducting
the chorus, she came up to me and asked if the boy whose hand she
held onto tightly, an orphan in her charge, could sing with us.
Those of us who heard the request were not eager for a children's
hour, but we could not say no to a nun and so we said all right. What

5

could he sing? How about the Bach-Gounod "Ave Maria?" she suggested.

The child—he was ten years old we learned, though he looked much younger—had a pure soprano voice, clear and vibrato-less. We were stunned, awed. He soared over our accompaniment, lifting us up with him. I had never heard anything like it, and Christian friends in the chorus said neither had they, though they had heard that two centuries ago a voice like that would have endangered the boy's manhood. Thirty-five years later that lovely sound still vibrates within me.

Weren't we lucky that neither Boss nor the school administration nor we realized that we were joined in a conspiracy to violate the Constitution of the United States?

Introduction

THE CURRENT CONTROVERSY over church-state relations in America, in particular the issues of prayers in public schools, governmental support of parochial schools, and displays in public places of religious symbols, is unfortunate and unnecessary.

The United States Supreme Court, whose decisions beginning in 1940 gave rise to the current controversy, seems at last to be aware of the mistake it made. Recent decisions of the Court have gone a long way to rectifying the problems and defusing the controversy. But the Court, which earned much of the public disapproval it received in recent years, now needs informed public support for its efforts to repair the damage it did in its series of misguided and confusing decisions involving the religion clauses of the First Amendment. Such support has not been forthcoming, neither from public officials issuing resounding calls for a constitutional amendment which would only usher in another generation of conflict over interpretation and application, nor from "strict separationists" demanding, with cool disdain for the desires of the overwhelming majority of Americans and with a sorry ignorance of American history, the complete exclusion of all forms of religious expression from public life.

The great mass of American people has watched the emotional debate with anxiety. They see the admirable and precious interfaith amiability of recent years disturbed by completely unnecessary lawsuits over issues as divisive as they are irrelevant to true religious freedom. To me, a Jew living in a country where almost everybody else is Christian, there is only one religious issue: equal treatment. If the New Testament is read in public schools, I want the Old Testament too. If Catholic parochial schools receive financial aid, I want yeshivas to get their fair share. If public employees get time off for Good Friday, I want them to get time off for Yom Kippur. If a crèche is displayed during the Christmas season on the lawn of the public library, I want to see a menorah nearby.

My position is hardly unduly modest. Imagine in almost any other country of the world a member of a religious group representing less than 3 percent of the population *demanding,* and with a fair chance of receiving, equal treatment with the dominant religion. And yet there are Americans—Jews, Unitarians, "humanists," atheists, even some Protestants—who believe I do not demand enough. They do not want equal time with their neighbors, they want absolute veto power over their neighbors' actions. As they do not wish their children to say prayers in public school, they insist that nobody else's be permitted to do so. As they do not send their children to parochial schools, they insist that no public aid be given such schools, although the parents of parochial school children are assessed for public school taxes at the same rate as everyone else. They are offended by any form of religious symbol in a public place and cannot be consoled with the right to erect their own there—especially if they do not have any.

We are a free country and there is no reason, apart from good taste and respect for the sensitivities of others, why a person so disposed should not lobby against the provision at public expense of textbooks to parochial schools. But to raise such a personal preference to constitutional status is wrong and dangerous. It invites a change in the Constitution, and we already have the most liberal constitution in the world, with greater protections for minorities than most nations dream of. We would be crazy to tamper with it.

But we cannot expect the vast majority of Americans to be willing to be governed by a document which a small minority is able to manipulate for its own benefit. Moreover, the supposed benefit is nonexistent, except for those who make their living conducting wasteful litigation. Barring Handel's *Messiah* from the public schools will have far less impact on the Christian child who can sing it in church than on the Jewish child who will thereby be "protected" from exposure to an important and enriching part of the culture of the Western world; and if crèches and menorahs are given comparable prominence in public displays, the prime beneficiary will be the menorah. FCC equal-time rules primarily benefit minority candidates.

The definitive proof that a strictly separationist posture does not really protect minorities is the fact that the Supreme Court, while holding that no one can pray or read the Bible *voluntarily* in a public school, has held that an Orthodox Jew can be *compelled* to observe the Christian sabbath and can be *prohibited* from wearing his yarmulka in the armed forces. Indeed, the Court has held that a state statute giving everyone the right to choose his own sabbath is unconstitutional: under the strict-separationist interpretation of the establishment clause, only the Christian sabbath can be enforced by the state.

But I am getting ahead of my story. There is an enormous gap between a generation which *in extremis* placed "firm reliance on the protection of Divine Providence" and one which fears the evil effects on kindergarten children of saying grace before their morning milk and cookies. How we got from one to the other, and how our courts came to "interpret" (*amend* would be more accurate) the Constitution, written in a spirit of liberal hope by the former, to institutionalize the narrow-minded fears of the latter, is the story upon which we are about to embark.

(At the back of this book are citations for every case mentioned in the text. They are organized in chronological order, as is the text. In most instances the referent textual material is obvious by date, state, or name of case. Where there might be uncertainty I have included a brief annotation. For readers unfamiliar with the form of legal citation I have appended a brief guide to legal research. With the aid of this guide any case cited in this book can easily be found.)

CHAPTER I

The Original Understanding

Congress shall make no law respecting an establishment of religion or prohibiting the free exercise thereof.

I N   T H E   B E G I N N I N G there was no tension between the "establishment" clause and the "free exercise" clause.

The meaning of "establishment" was clear when the Bill of Rights was proposed, debated and adopted. Six of the original thirteen states—Connecticut, Georgia, Maryland, Massachusetts, New Hampshire and South Carolina—had officially supported churches. It was understood, and these six states would not have entered the Union under any other understanding, that the new federal government would not attempt to interfere with these arrangements. At the same time there were states, led by Jefferson's Virginia, which separated secular and ecclesiastical functions rather strictly and did not want the federal government to interfere with the arrangements they had worked out. It was universally agreed, by the states with subsidized churches and the states with more or less high walls of separation (Jefferson's metaphor) between church and state, that the federal government was to be absolutely forbidden to establish a national church.

There were thus two aspects to the establishment clause: (1) no interference with state church-state relations, and (2) no establishment of a national church; and there was virtually no disagreement over either of these purposes of the establishment clause of the First Amendment. Few if any provisions of the Constitution were less controversial.

It was equally agreed that, just as the federal government should be prohibited from telling the people how to worship, it should be prohibited from telling them how not to worship. A large number of the American people had come to the New World for the primary purpose of being able to worship without governmental restraint. They had not fled from royal persecutions of Catholics or Huguenots or Quakers or Jews or whatever only to substitute democratically elected inquisitors. The federal government must be absolutely prohibited from interfering with the free exercise by each citizen of his religion.

Actually, there was one controversial aspect of the religion clauses of the First Amendment: many people thought them unnecessary. The federal government was to be a government of enumerated powers, exercising only those powers expressly accorded it by the Constitution. As no powers over religious affairs were given it by the Constitution, there was no way, it was argued, that the federal government could ever assume such powers. The one potential area of uncertainty—religious tests for public office —was dealt with in the body of the Constitution by means of an explicit prohibition. A century before anything comparable existed even in England, no American had to violate his conscience in order to take his seat in the national legislature. Nevertheless, keeping the federal government out of religious affairs was so important to the people setting up that government that the first sentence of the first amendment to the Constitution provided that "Congress shall make no law respecting an establishment of religion or prohibiting the free exercise thereof."

That did not mean that anarchy reigned in the area of church-state relations, any more than it did where murder, rape, marriage and divorce, or the title to real property was concerned. Those were matters within the province of state and local governments which, after all, were fully developed and operating when the federal government was created. And the states themselves had constitutions which, to the extent the people wished, restricted the actions of state legislatures just as the Constitution of the United States restricted the actions of Congress. Had the people of any state so desired, and many did, to establish a church or to prohibit a church establishment, they were free to do so—and many did. Indeed, to this day, and this seems sometimes to be forgotten by opponents of Supreme Court decisions in the area of school prayers and aid to parochial schools, many state constitutions are more strictly separationist than the federal Constitution.

But it never occurred to anyone that in prohibiting the federal government from interfering in church-state relations, the First Amendment would have any effect at all on state activities in that area. In the words of Chief Justice John Marshall, perhaps the greatest jurist in American history:

> Had the people of the several states, or any of them, required changes in their constitutions, had they required additional safeguards to liberty from the apprehended encroachments of their particular governments, the remedy was in their own hands, and would have been applied by themselves. The unwieldy and cumbrous machinery of procuring a recommendation from two-thirds of Congress, and the assent of three-fourths of their sister states, could never have occurred to any human being as a mode of doing that which might be effected by the state itself.

In view of subsequent history, it should perhaps be noted that no one expected the federal government to be hostile to religion. In its own proper sphere, where its own affairs were concerned, it was naturally assumed that the federal government would maintain friendly relations with the various faiths represented by its members. Thus the first Congress, which proposed the Bill of Rights, appointed chaplains at the outset of its first session. It also appointed chaplains for the armed forces and resolved that George Washington's inaugural should culminate in a divine service at St. Paul's chapel, an Anglican church. Indeed, on the very day that it approved the First Amendment the Congress called upon President Washington to proclaim a day of "public thanksgiving and prayer." Sessions of the United States Supreme Court were, as they still are, commenced with a prayer that "God save the United States and this honorable Court."

The federal government was forbidden to interfere with the people's religious life. It was not required to abandon its own.

As for religious toleration, the results could not have been better. By mid-century, all the state establishments had been dismantled. Americans were by far the freest people in the world in their religious lives. Pockets of intolerance continued to exist here and there, to be sure. But precisely because church-state relations were a local concern, progress could be achieved without confrontations on the national level; and in extreme cases members of a persecuted minority could seek a more congenial community without having to abandon their country.

One issue did become a national issue, and it tore the country apart. The fatal flaw of the system was the failure of the Founding Fathers to deal with the sin and shame of slavery. Their failure resulted from the fact that, in contrast with the general agreement over the role of government in religion, there was no consensus regarding slavery. The best efforts of perhaps the most resourceful and wisest generation of men who ever lived accordingly resulted in a pitiful compromise whereby for purposes of representation and taxation a slave counted as three-fifths of a human being, and after twenty years Congress could prohibit the slave trade. But no protections for slaves were included in the Constitution or the Bill of Rights and their ultimate manumission was not even officially contemplated.

This is obviously not the place to recount the struggle over slavery. What is relevant is that after the Civil War three amendments to the Constitution were passed which expressly limited the powers of the states. The Thirteenth Amendment abolished slavery. The Fifteenth Amendment gave all citizens of the United States, regardless of race "or previous condition of servitude," the right to vote. The third Civil War Amendment, the Fourteenth, required each state to treat all persons within its jurisdiction on an equal basis. It provided that:

No State shall make or enforce any law which shall abridge the privileges or immunities of citizens of the United States; nor shall any State deprive any person of life, liberty, or property, without due process of law; nor deny to any person within its jurisdiction the equal protection of the laws.

As we shall see, it was this Amendment which the Supreme Court ultimately used to extend the religion clauses of the First Amendment to the states. Surprisingly, it was not the "privileges and immunities" clause or even the "equal protection" clause that the Court fastened upon, but the "due process" clause. But that was much later. At the time, religion was not mentioned or thought of in connection with any of the Civil War Amendments.

Religion was not mentioned in the Civil War Amendments for the excellent reason that there was no religious issue in the Civil War. There was a religious issue afterward. President Grant was an adherent of the most complete separation between church and state. He was not satisfied that the Constitution kept the federal government out of the religious affairs of the people; he wanted the states to be subjected to a similar prohibition. In the last year of his administration, an amendment was introduced in the Congress to accomplish this purpose. Known for its proposer in the House, James G. Blaine, who eight years later would be Republican candidate for President, the Blaine Amendment would have extended the religious clauses of the First Amendment to the states and, for good measure, have added a prohibition of aid to parochial schools.

The House passed the Blaine Amendment and sent it to the Senate where it was proposed by Senator Frelinghuysen, former Attorney General of New Jersey and a leader of the Congress which had passed the Fourteenth Amendment. Senator Frelinghuysen noted that the First Amendment was "an inhibition on Congress, and not on the States." He continued:

> The [Blaine Amendment] very properly extends the prohibition of the first amendment of the Constitution to the States. Thus the [Blaine Amendment] prohibits the States, for the first time, from the establishment of religion, from prohibiting its free exercise, and from making any religious test a qualification to office.

Senator Eaton of Connecticut found the Blaine Amendment offensive. "I am opposed," he said, "to any State prohibiting the free exercise of any religion; and I do not require the Senate or the Congress of the United States to assist me in taking care of the State of Connecticut in that regard." Senator Whyte agreed: "The first amendment to the Constitution prevents the establishment of religion by congressional enactment; it prohibits the interference of Congress with the free exercise thereof, and leaves the whole power for the propagation of it with the States exclusively; and so far as I am concerned I propose to leave it there also."

In other words, both proponents and opponents of the Blaine Amendment agreed that nothing in the Constitution prohibited the states from establishing a religion or from interfering with the free exercise thereof. Certainly no one imagined that the Fourteenth Amendment had extended the religion clauses of the First Amendment to the states. As many members of the Congress which considered the Blaine Amendment had sat in the Congress which voted for the Fourteenth Amendment seven years earlier, it is unlikely they overlooked its possible significance.

The Blaine Amendment did not receive the necessary votes in the Senate. For the next half century it was reintroduced in Congress after Congress. It never passed. It was not abandoned, however, until the Supreme Court, by judicial fiat, made it superfluous.

CHAPTER II

The First Breach

T HE BLAINE AMENDMENT was proposed, and
defeated, in 1876. For the next half century it remained clear
that church-state relations in America were exclusively a state concern. In 1884, for example, the Supreme Court of Iowa held that
Bible reading, recitation of the Lord's Prayer, and singing of religious songs in the public schools of Iowa did not violate the constitution of Iowa, in 1890 the Supreme Court of Wisconsin held that
Bible reading in the public schools of Wisconsin did not violate the
constitution of that state, in 1898 the Supreme Court of Michigan
held that Bible reading in the public schools of that state did not
violate its constitution, in 1902 the Supreme Court of Nebraska
held that Bible reading and singing religious songs in public schools
violated that state's constitution, in 1904 the Supreme Court of
Kansas held that reading the Lord's Prayer and the Twenty-Third
Psalm in public schools did not violate the constitution of Kansas,
and also in 1904 the Supreme Court of Kentucky held that Bible
reading and prayer in public schools did not violate the constitution
of Kentucky. In none of these cases, neither the ones in which
religious activities in public schools were upheld nor the ones in

which they were struck down, was the Constitution of the United States even mentioned.

In 1908, the United States Supreme Court had occasion to reaffirm the inapplicability of the Bill of Rights to state action in a case involving the Fifth Amendment privilege against self-incrimination. In an opinion which forty years later Supreme Court Justice and former Harvard Law School Professor Felix Frankfurter would hail as "the judicial process at its best . . . one of the outstanding opinions in the history of the Court," the Court reviewed the series of cases in which the states were held not bound by the right to bear arms guaranteed by the Second Amendment, the right to a grand jury indictment guaranteed by the Fifth Amendment, the Sixth Amendment right to be confronted by one's accusers, or the Seventh Amendment right to trial by jury in civil cases. The Court noted that some eminent persons had expressed the view that the Fourteenth Amendment due process clause had made the Bill of Rights applicable to the states but, in the light of this unbroken series of cases, "the question is no longer open in this court."

That did not mean, the Court was quick to add, that none of the rights enumerated in the Bill of Rights could be enforced against state action. It did mean that merely because the federal government was prohibited from doing something by the Bill of Rights did not mean that the states were subject to a similar prohibition. The test under the due process clause, which the Fourteenth Amendment had extended to the states, was: "Is it a fundamental principle of liberty and justice which inheres in the very idea of free government and is it the inalienable right of a citizen of such a government?" If a claimed right were such a fundamental principle, then due process required the states as well as the federal government to respect it; but not otherwise.

In the case at bar, the defendants had been convicted of forging bank records. At their trial in a New Jersey state court they had failed to testify, which was their right under New Jersey law. But the trial judge, as was *his* right under New Jersey law, had instructed the jury that they were free to draw unfavorable inferences from the defendants' silence, and evidently the jury had. The defendants argued in the United States Supreme Court that the result of this procedure was that they had in effect been made to incriminate themselves and that this violated the Fifth Amendment prohibition against involuntary self-incrimination.

Had the defendants been convicted in a federal court, the Supreme Court would have had to answer the rather interesting question of whether the privilege against self-incrimination is violated when a jury is allowed to notice a defendant taking advantage of it. But the Court never reached that question, for it decided that the privilege against self-incrimination was not enforceable against state action. It was not "a fundamental principle of liberty and justice which inheres in the very idea of free government," as shown by the fact that many civilized countries did not recognize a blanket right to avoid self-incrimination, that a respectable body of opinion in the United States felt that the privilege was probably unnecessary and surely abused, and that, addressing the specific instance before the Court, many eminently civilized countries permitted the trial judge to comment on the failure of a criminal defendant to testify on his own behalf.

The Court had not mentioned religion, which was in no way involved in the case. But if the privilege against self-incrimination contained in the Fifth Amendment was not "a fundamental principle of liberty and justice which inheres in the very idea of free government," then surely the establishment clause of the First Amendment was not. After all, most countries had established churches, including England, which many people looked to as the epitome of a free country; and, as noted, six American states had subsidized churches at the time the Constitution came into effect.

In any event, state courts continued to hold that the religion clauses of the First Amendment were not applicable to state action. In 1908, for example, two Roman Catholics, two Jews, and one person who "does not believe in the inspiration of the Bible," sued their school board in Texas to stop the reading in the public schools of the King James version of the Bible, the recitation of the Lord's prayer, and the singing of hymns. The children were not required to participate, most Biblical passages were taken from the Old Testament, and when a rabbi complained about certain of the songs being prepared for a Christmas pageant, the superintendent of schools, according to his testimony, "had it stopped." The Supreme Court of Texas found no violation of the state constitution in these activities. There was no reference to the federal Constitution.

Two years later, in Illinois, two Roman Catholics objected to the reading in the public schools of the King James Bible, which they deemed "incorrect and incomplete," to the version of the Lord's Prayer being used, and indeed to the entire idea of having devotional exercises in the public schools. The Supreme Court of Illinois agreed with them and, in an eloquent, impassioned opinion, held that such activities were clearly violative of the Illinois constitution. Two justices disagreed and dissented on the ground that the Bible, in whatever version, could not be deemed sectarian. But all the justices agreed that the federal Constitution, which the plaintiffs had invoked, was inapplicable. In the words of the court, "That instrument contains no restrictions in this respect upon the Legislatures of the states, which are thus left free to enact such laws in respect of religion as they may deem proper, restrained only by the limitations of the respective state Constitutions."

In 1915, the Supreme Court of Louisiana held that the reading of passages from the New Testament in public schools attended by Jewish children "infringes on [their] religious scruples" and therefore violated the constitution of Louisiana. In 1922, the Supreme Court of Georgia held that a municipal ordinance which required the daily reading in public schools of passages from the King James version of the Old or New Testament, and which also provided that any child who objected should be excused, did not violate the constitution of Georgia. In neither case was the federal Constitution mentioned.

In 1922, the United States Supreme Court reaffirmed yet again that the Fourteenth Amendment did not automatically incorporate the Bill of Rights and make every clause of it applicable to the states. A Missouri statute provided that a corporation doing business in the state must, upon the request of a former employee, furnish him with a letter stating the reasons for the termination of his employment. Cheek, a former Prudential employee, requested such a letter, was refused, and lodged a complaint under the statute. Prudential defended on the ground that the statute violated its freedom of speech and its correlative right to remain silent. The Supreme Court held that freedom of speech, contained in the First

Amendment, was applicable only to the federal government. "Neither the Fourteenth Amendment nor any provision of the Constitution of the United States," the Court held, "imposes upon the States any restrictions about 'freedom of speech' . . . ."

But in that same year, Oregon, by public referendum, passed a statute requiring all children between the ages of eight and sixteen to attend public school. Only children with physical or mental handicaps requiring special education were excepted. No exception was made for children attending religious schools or any other kinds of private school. The statute threatened the imminent destruction of every non-public school in the state.

A Catholic school and a private military academy sued. The United States Supreme Court found that "The inevitable practical result of enforcing the act under consideration would be destruction of appellees' primary schools, and perhaps all other private primary schools for normal children within the state of Oregon," and voided the statute.

A simple case. A state attempted the destruction of private property with what the courts found a lack of due process, and the courts protected the property. An everyday case with no hint of a constitutional revolution. No religious issue was decided or even raised, although one of the plaintiffs was a parochial school. No religious issue could, for the reasons already adumbrated, be raised in a federal court. Thus the Court did not consider whether the Oregon statute interfered with the free exercise rights of Catholics or whether an exemption for Catholics would have constituted an impermissible establishment of religion. No such issue was before the Court—indeed, no Catholic parent or child was before the Court. The only issue was whether a profitable business, which had committed no wrong, could be destroyed overnight by state action. Noting that "this court has gone very far to protect against loss threatened by such action," the Supreme Court said it could not be.

But, in passing, the Court expressed the opinion that "we think it entirely plain that the [statute] unreasonably interferes with the liberty of parents and guardians to direct the upbringing and education of children under their control." By reason of this affirmation of a "liberty" nowhere mentioned in the Constitution nor theretofore heard of, belonging to persons not before the Court, this case became known as establishing a constitutional right for parents to send their children to private schools. Indeed, although there was no religious issue in the case, and although one of the two plaintiffs was a non-religious school, the case became known as establishing a constitutional right for parents to send their children to religious schools. Thus in 1972, when the Supreme Court held that Amish parents had a constitutional right to withdraw their children from school at fourteen, notwithstanding a state compulsory education statute requiring schooling until sixteen, Chief Justice Burger wrote: "However read, the Court's holding in [the Oregon case] stands as a charter of the rights of parents to direct the religious upbringing of their children."

No medieval alchemist ever dreamed of a more dramatic transformation of a base metal into gold. But the process had only been begun in 1925, when the Oregon case was decided, and its broader implications seem not yet to have been perceived.

CHAPTER III

Hard Cases Make Bad Law

W ORLD WAR I culminated in Communist governments in Russia, Hungary, and parts of Germany. Worldwide Communist takeovers seemed a real possibility. In response, many American states passed "criminal anarchy" and "criminal syndicalism" statutes to defend themselves against the red peril (and, incidentally, to defend their businessmen against increasingly energetic efforts to organize labor).

Benjamin Gitlow was a member of a breakaway left-wing faction of the Socialist Party of America. He was business manager of the official newspaper of this radical faction and largely responsible for its first issue, which called for a "Communist revolution" by means of strikes and other "revolutionary mass action" leading to a "revolutionary dictatorship of the proletariat." He was duly prosecuted and convicted under New York's "criminal anarchy" statute which made it a crime to advocate "overthrowing or overturning organized government by force or violence."

Gitlow's conviction was affirmed by the New York courts. He appealed to the United States Supreme Court, arguing that New York's "criminal anarchy" statute violated his freedom of speech and press guaranteed by the First Amendment.

As we have seen, the Supreme Court had squarely held that the guarantee of free speech contained in the First Amendment was applicable to the federal government only, not to the states. But the Court was appalled by the vague and shadowy, and infinitely extensible, criminal anarchy and syndicalism statutes sprouting like mushrooms all over the country and threatening to make a mockery of the very concept of free expression. Faced with such a possibility the Court realized that, contrary to what it had held only three years before, free speech and press "are among the fundamental personal rights and 'liberties' protected by the due process clause of the Fourteenth Amendment from impairment by the States." The Court therefore held, unanimously, that henceforward the guarantees of free speech and press were applicable to state action. It dealt with the prior case with the laconic remark that "We do not regard the incidental statement in [that case] that the Fourteenth Amendment imposes no restrictions on the States concerning freedom of speech, as determinative of this question."

A great victory for Gitlow's lawyer, but not for Gitlow, whose conviction the Court affirmed. What the Court had done was to give fair warning to the states to clean up their act or face federal intervention on whatever grounds the Court might find ready to hand. But that did not mean that it wished to give a Communist organizer carte blanche to subvert orderly government in America. Gitlow went to jail.

Within months the Court was faced with a case under a comparable California statute. This made it a crime to belong to an organization which advocated the use of unlawful means for "accomplishing a change in industrial ownership or control, or effecting any political change." The net was spreading wider, making mere membership in a suspect organization, presumably even without active participation in any unlawful activities, a crime. Now the Court added freedom of assembly to the First Amendment guarantees applicable to the states, although again it affirmed the conviction of the defendant for being a member and officer of the Communist Party of America.

Justices Holmes and Brandeis, two of the greatest jurists ever to sit on the Supreme Court, concurred in the judgment of the Court but, in an opinion by Brandeis, made manifest their growing disquiet over the sweeping scope and potential for oppression in statutes designed, as these statutes patently were, to suppress ideas and associations. In the course of his concurring opinion, Brandeis came close to admitting that it was precisely his revulsion at this type of legislation which had led him to accept the "incorporation doctrine" whereby provisions of the Bill of Rights were extended to the states via the due process clause of the Fourteenth amendment. "Despite arguments to the contrary which had seemed to me persuasive," Brandeis candidly wrote, "it is settled that the due process clause of the Fourteenth Amendment applies to matter of substantive law as well as to matters of procedure. Thus all fundamental rights comprised within the term liberty are protected by the Federal Constitution from invasion by the States."

Thus the Court announced to the country that it was now prepared to assume power over state action in areas where it had previously held it lacked the power to do so. While these cases dealt only with First Amendment guarantees of free speech, press, and association, the same rationale was certainly available to extend the reach of the other clauses of the Bill of Rights and, incidentally, of the powers of the federal courts.

But note the manner in which the Court accomplished this judicial revolution. In each case the Court declared itself possessed of a new, extraordinary power—and then declined to exercise it. This was precisely the mechanism used by Chief Justice Marshall in 1803 when he assumed for the Court its most far-reaching power, the power to declare acts of Congress unconstitutional. In that famous case—Marbury v. Madison, probably the most important judicial decision in the history of American jurisprudence—Marshall held that an act of Congress which empowered the Court to issue writs of mandamus to officers of the executive branch requiring them to perform some public duty was unconstitutional because no such power was conferred on the Court by the Constitution. Of course the Constitution also conferred no power of judicial review on the Court, but since the immediate effect of the decision in Marbury v. Madison was to permit the executive branch to do what it wanted to do without interference from the Court, it was difficult for anyone to contest Marshall's breathtaking assumption of that power for the future. For similar reasons the long-range impact of the first two criminal anarchy cases decided by the Court was barely noticed at the time.

But in 1931, another anti-Red case reached the Supreme Court, and this time it felt constrained to reverse the conviction. Again the case originated in California, where a statute made it a crime to display a red flag if a jury should find that it symbolized advocacy of the violent overthrow of the government. Under this statute a nineteen-year-old girl was tried and convicted for raising a red flag at a Young Communist summer camp. (Had the prosecutor wanted to kill the statute, he could hardly have chosen a better case with which to do it.) Chief Justice Charles Evans Hughes, a conservative member of the Eastern Establishment who had been Republican candidate for President in 1916, and whose revulsion for subversive activities could hardly be questioned, found the statute "repugnant to the guaranty of liberty contained in the Fourteenth Amendment." The conviction was reversed.

A few years later the Court, in yet another anti-Red case, had the opportunity to summarize the relationship between the Fourteenth Amendment and the Bill of Rights. The defendant had been tried and convicted of violating an Oregon criminal syndicalism statute. He had attended and spoken at a meeting sponsored by the Communist Party. Though the state conceded that neither the defendant nor anyone else at the meeting had said anything unlawful, he was sentenced to *eight years* in jail—significantly more than he would have gotten for, say, armed robbery. By unanimous decision the Supreme Court reversed the conviction. Chief Justice Hughes wrote:

> Freedom of speech and of the press are fundamental rights which are safeguarded by the due process clause of the Fourteenth Amendment of the Federal Constitution. The right of peaceable assembly is a right cognate to those of free speech and free press and is equally fundamental. It follows . . . that . . . peaceable assembly for lawful discussion cannot be made a crime.

But later that same year, the Court indicated that it was not yet ready to effect a wholesale incorporation of the Bill of Rights into the Fourteenth Amendment.

The defendant had been found guilty after trial in a Connecticut state court of second degree murder and been given the maximum sentence for that crime, life imprisonment. But the prosecutor was not satisfied. As he believed the trial judge had made errors of law which had converted a murder first conviction into a murder second, he invoked a rather unusual Connecticut statute and appealed the verdict. A Connecticut appellate court ordered a new trial, though the defendant argued that he was thereby being placed in double jeopardy in violation of the Fifth Amendment. He was retried, found guilty of first degree murder, and sentenced to die.

Now, one might think that protection against multiple trials for the same offense was at least as essential an aspect of liberty as being free to raise a red flag at summer camp. The Court did not think so. Justice Cardozo, writing for the Court, paraphrased the defendant's argument in this way: "Whatever would be a violation of the original bill of rights if done by the federal government is now equally unlawful by force of the Fourteenth Amendment if done by a state." To this argument Cardozo replied, "There is no such general rule." Only those provisions of the Bill of Rights which are "implicit in the concept of ordered liberty" were applicable to the states via the due process clause of the Fourteenth Amendment. Since the prohibition of double jeopardy did not so qualify, the defendant could be executed.

But the camel was in the tent from nose to tail and before long Cardozo's "There is no such general rule" would be obsolete.

CHAPTER IV

The Federal Takeover of Religion

I N 1927, T H E Supreme Court of Minnesota held that the reading in public schools of passages from the King James version of the Old Testament did not violate the constitution of Minnesota. Neither the opinion of the court nor the strong dissenting opinion mentioned the federal Constitution.

In 1929, the Supreme Court of South Dakota held that the expulsion of Roman Catholic children from public school for refusing to attend readings of the King James Bible violated their rights under the South Dakota Constitution. Two justices dissented and wrote long, discursive opinions. No one mentioned the federal Constitution.

In 1930, the Supreme Court of the State of Washington denied a petition to compel the state board of education to require Bible readings in the public schools. Apart from the expressed reluctance of the court to interfere in educational policies better left to the discretion of the school board, (*autre temps, autre moeurs*), the court noted that it had already held that Bible readings in public schools violated the constitution of Washington. If the petitioners wished to change the law in this regard, the court added, they "may direct their efforts toward amending the [state] Constitution." While no mention was made of the federal Constitution, it was implicit in the court's advice that an amendment of the state constitution would suffice, that the federal Constitution would not stand in the way.

In 1936, the Supreme Court of North Dakota held that nuns could wear habits while teaching in public schools without offending the constitution of North Dakota. The court expressly held that the federal Constitution did not apply to state actions concerning religion.

Then came Justice Cardozo's opinion in the double jeopardy case where the Supreme Court held that the guarantee against multiple trials for the same offense was not applicable to the states. And then came the Jehovah's Witnesses.

There were about 60,000 Witnesses in the United States in the 1930s, but they made up in aggressive activity what they lacked in numbers. Each Witness was deemed by his coreligionists an ordained minister with a duty to proselytize among the heathen (all non-Witnesses) and to persuade them to become Witnesses before the onset of Armageddon, which was imminent. They were disciplined, conscientious, courageous, oblivious of anyone else's rights or sensitivities, and exceedingly unpopular.

They were not welcomed in the cities and towns across America where they came in groups to spread their Word and to denounce, often in the most offensive terms, everyone else's. In particular they excoriated the Catholic Church, which they called a "great racket," a "harlot," a "whore." In self-defense, and to forestall their citizens from committing mayhem or murder, many communities passed anti-Witness laws—usually couched euphemistically in general terms as laws designed to control "peddling" or "use of the public streets" or "solicitation of funds"—and also arrested Witness evangels for disturbing the peace or desecrating the Sabbath, of all of which they were manifestly and proudly guilty.

The Witnesses took their persecutors to court, for which enterprise they had a well-financed and competent legal department, an unlimited supply of willing plaintiffs, and no choice, for their small numbers and great unpopularity rendered them powerless to influence legislative action. But they lost every case they brought on free exercise grounds. Then they changed their legal tactics, claimed that ordinances prohibiting or restricting the dissemination of ideas by written or spoken word violated their freedom of press and speech, and won a case.

An ordinance in Griffin, Georgia, prohibited the distribution of books, pamphlets, or other written material without a license. A Witness was convicted of violating the ordinance when he distributed religious tracts without the requisite license, and when he refused to pay a fine, he was sentenced to jail. The Supreme Court struck down the ordinance as void on its face. Speaking for an unanimous Court, Chief Justice Hughes wrote that "it strikes at the very foundation of the freedom of the press by subjecting it to license and censorship." The fact that the appellant was distributing religious tracts was irrelevant—freedom of the press was the only constitutional provision cited, and the Chief Justice traced the history of that freedom all the way back to the time of John Milton.

Next year the Court held that ordinances in Los Angeles, Milwaukee, and Worcester, Massachusetts, which prohibited the distribution of leaflets on public streets, and an ordinance in Irvington, New Jersey, which prohibited door-to-door canvassing, were all impermissible restrictions on freedom of speech and press. The fact that in one of the cases a Witness was involved was not material—in the other three cases the defendants had been distributing political literature.

As of 1940—more than 150 years after the Constitution came into effect, more than seventy years after the adoption of the Fourteenth Amendment—the religion clauses of the First Amendment had never been extended to the states. The new era began on May 29, 1940.

Newton Cantwell and his sons Russell, 18, and Jesse, 16, were Jehovah's Witnesses. In the spring of 1938 they brought their message to New Haven, Connecticut.

New Haven is internationally known as the home of Yale University, and many people have seen photographs and paintings of that great university's Oxford-like gothic buildings and sheltered quadrangles. Less well known are New Haven's many rundown neighborhoods whose decaying housing stock is inhabited by the submerged minority of the moment. In 1938, one such minority were the Irish Catholics who lived in what the Supreme Court came to describe as "a thickly populated neighborhood" but which *Time* magazine portrayed more vividly as "a lean and hungry district." It was 90 percent Catholic, and the Cantwells chose it as a likely place to practice their ministry.

They brought with them a book called *Enemies* and a phonograph record that described it. They collared two Catholic men, John Ganley and John Cafferty, and played the record for them on a portable phonograph. This is what they heard:

> This book submits the conclusive proof that for more than 1,500 years a great religious system, operating out of Rome, has by means of fraud and deception brought untold sorrow and suffering on the people. It operates the greatest racket ever employed amongst men and robs the people of their money and destroys their peace of mind and freedom of action.

John Ganley and John Cafferty did not hear this exposé of their religion with the equanimity which the Cantwells might have encountered had they played their record to members of Yale's philosophy department. Nevertheless, they might have fared much worse than they did, for their unwilling auditors were law-abiding men who, in lieu of beating the Cantwells to a pulp, called the police.

The Cantwells were arrested and charged with violating a city ordinance which prohibited the solicitation of funds "for any alleged religious, charitable or philanthropic cause," except from members of one's own organization, without a license. The ordinance provided that a license would be issued to any organization which the city licensing authority found was a bona fide religious, charitable or philanthropic institution which "conforms to reasonable standards of efficiency and integrity." The Cantwells were also charged, on better evidence it would seem, with inciting a breach of the peace.

They were convicted on both charges. Actually, solicitation of funds was a small part of their activities, quite incidental to their main purpose, which was to spread their religious message by oral and written word. They did offer literature for sale, but they often gave it away when someone declined to pay for it, and they did

accept funds for their organization in the rare instance when someone offered a donation. But the amounts they collected were insignificant. Inciting to a breach of the peace was another matter, but
in fact they did not want Ganley and Cafferty to become violent;
they were not *trying* to create a public disturbance.

Of course they appealed. The oral argument in the Supreme
Court suggested an irreconcilability of views which boded ill for
domestic tranquillity. Chief Justice Hughes asked the Witnesses'
attorney:

"'I suppose these Catholics had some right of religious freedom
themselves, did they not? I suppose they have the right to be left
alone and not to be attacked with these scurrilous denunciations of
their most cherished faith. What have you to say to that?"

The Witness attorney replied:
"I say we are right."

The attorney for the state of Connecticut took a position which
seemed remarkable for a Christian. When he argued that it was and
ought to be unlawful "to stir up strife and discontent," Justice
McReynolds noted that Jesus had stirred up "a good deal of trouble
in Jerusalem." The state's counsel shot back: "As I remember my
Bible, something was done about that."

All of this was too much for the Court. It reversed the Cantwells'
conviction and, though it could readily have based its decision on
freedom of speech and press, it decided to face the religious issue
directly. The Court held:

The First Amendment declares that Congress shall make no law
respecting an establishment of religion or prohibiting the free exercise thereof. The Fourteenth Amendment has rendered the legislatures of the states as incompetent as Congress to enact such laws.

There was no establishment issue in the case. Thus, with respect
to the establishment clause of the First Amendment, the Court's
unqualified language only amounted to "dictum" — that is, a comment which, since it addressed an issue not before the Court, was

not binding on future courts. But the handwriting was surely on the wall.

But the United States Supreme Court was about to be split apart by two little children, a ten-year-old boy and a twelve-year-old girl, two devout Christian children who feared eternal damnation if they saluted the American flag.

CHAPTER V

A Child Shall Lead Them

————

THERE WERE EIGHT thousand people in 1935 in the depressed city of Minersville, tucked away in the anthracite hills of eastern Pennsylvania. Most of them were Roman Catholic, but for four years Walter Gobitis had been a Witness. Even so he was generally liked and his self-service grocery made him a respectable if modest living.

In 1935, two of the Gobitis children, ten-year-old William and twelve-year-old Lillian, were in the Minersville public schools, in the fifth and seventh grades. Like all other children in their school, indeed like all children in every American school, they began each day by saluting the American flag and reciting the Pledge of Allegiance—which, by the way, did not then invoke the name of God (that was added by Congress in 1954). Then it was revealed to the leadership of their church that the flag was a graven image which Exodus 20:4–5 forbade them to bow down before or serve. All Witnesses were accordingly ordered to abstain from the flag salute ceremony.

Forthwith, Witness children around the country, in a display of obedience which non-Witness parents might well have looked upon with wistful admiration, declined to participate in the flag salute ceremony. In lieu thereof they offered to give the following pledge:

> I have pledged my unqualified allegiance and devotion to Jehovah, the Almighty God, and to his Kingdom, for which Jesus commands all Christians to pray. I respect the flag of the United States and acknowledge it as a symbol of freedom and justice to all. I pledge allegiance and obedience to all the laws of the United States that are consistent with God's law, as set forth in the Bible.

Many communities were sympathetic and conciliatory. After all, Witness children were not in any way disruptive. Quite the contrary, they tended to be especially obedient and orderly children who only asked to be permitted to stand mute while the rest of the class recited the official Pledge of Allegiance, or to give their own pledge. But in Pennsylvania, which was perhaps the most hostile state to the Witnesses, there was little attempt at accommodation. The Gobitis children were expelled from school. They were then sent to a Witness school thirty miles outside Minersville, but Walter Gobitis, who had three other children of preschool age, was already feeling the financial strain and decided to fight.

With the help of Witness counsel and the American Civil Liberties Union Gobitis filed suit in the United States District Court for the Eastern District of Pennsylvania. He sought an injunction requiring the school authorities of Minersville to take his children back and exempt them from the flag salute requirement. The District Judge, a Roosevelt appointee and a Quaker, found for Gobitis, holding that only the gravest danger to the public could justify any abridgment of free exercise rights and that "the refusal of these two earnest Christian children to salute the flag cannot even remotely prejudice or imperil the safety, health, morals, property or personal rights of their fellows."

The decision was not acceptable to the school board of Minersville. Poor as the district was, it found the money, with the help of the Improved Order of Red Men, the Patriotic Order of the Sons of America, and the Order of Independent Americans, to appeal the order to the United States Court of Appeals for the Third Circuit. That court affirmed unanimously. But the school board and its friends evidently had limitless time and money to spend, and the determination to spend it, to make the Gobitis children conform or stay out of the public schools. It filed a petition for certiorari in the United States Supreme Court and, though the Court only grants a few of the petitions submitted to it, this petition was granted.

In the Supreme Court, briefs urging affirmance were filed on behalf of the Gobitis children by the ACLU and the Bill of Rights Committee of the American Bar Association, but the case continued to be handled directly by the Witnesses' legal department. They had, after all, already won two rounds of the legal battle without a single dissent. But a power struggle within the Witness leadership led to the dismissal of the lawyer who had successfully guided their efforts in the District and Circuit courts. The case was taken over by a national leader of the Witnesses who was a member of the bar but who was far more interested in the Word than in the law—or than in the Gobitis children. At oral argument in the Supreme Court he treated the Justices to a theological tirade which quite alienated them and in general abandoned the legal strategies which had worked so well for his predecessor.

In the conference room after the argument there seemed to be unanimous agreement for reversal. Chief Justice Hughes selected Justice Felix Frankfurter, a former professor at Harvard Law School and a close personal friend of President Roosevelt, to write the opinion of the Court. As Frankfurter did not need to worry about holding together a wavering majority he was able to give unrestrained vent to his fervent patriotism. "The ultimate foundation of a free society," wrote the Jewish immigrant from a Germany then in the throes of the Hitlerite madness:

> is the binding tie of cohesive sentiment. Such a sentiment is fostered by all those agencies of the mind and spirit which may serve to gather up the traditions of a people, transmit them from generation to generation, and thereby create that continuity of a treasured common life which constitutes a civilization. "We live by symbols." The flag is a symbol of our national unity.

Frankfurter's opinion, which is worth reading in its entirety for its eloquence and its deep patriotic passion, was warmly applauded by his colleagues. Justice William Douglas, one of the great liberals on the Court, wrote to Frankfurter: "This is a powerful, moving document of incalculable contemporary and (I believe) historic value. I congratulate you on a truly statesmanlike job." Justice Roberts called it "among the best ever prepared by a judge of this Court." Justice Murphy, the only Catholic on the Court and a man whose own religious convictions were strongly held, was deeply troubled by the case—he called it his Gethsemane—but congratulated Frankfurter on a "beautifully expressed opinion."

But Justice Harlan Fiske Stone, who within one year would be Chief Justice, was not swept away by the force of Frankfurter's eloquence. When Frankfurter's opinion was circulated among the Justices for signature Stone declined to sign; and, although he had not spoken up at the post-argument conference, he now advised his brethren that he intended to file a dissenting opinion. On decision day, after Frankfurter read his opinion, Stone read, with great emotion:

> There are other ways to teach loyalty and patriotism, which are the sources of national unity, than by compelling the pupil to affirm that which he does not believe and by commanding a form of affirmance which violates his religious convictions.

But the Gobitis children lost, eight to one. The impact of the decision was immediate and widespread. "The wave of anti-Witness persecution which swept the country after the Gobitis decision," wrote the chief historian of the Witnesses' constitutional struggles, "is legendary." Mob violence against the unpopular Witnesses, often connived in by the police, had been widespread even before the decision, but it seemed to give Witness-baiting an imprimatur of respectability and even a patina of patriotism. In Maine, a virtual pogrom was put down only when the governor threatened to send in the National Guard. Witnesses were beaten and their cars burned in Illinois, Wyoming, Mississippi, and Nebraska. In Arkansas, a Witness convention was invaded by a mob armed with pipes and guns. In Oregon, a mob of a thousand people attacked a Witness meeting hall. In Maryland, the police openly joined a mob in breaking up a Witness meeting. In West Virginia, whose contribution to the flag salute controversy would within three years exceed Minersville's, Witnesses were detained by the police and, while in police custody, following a procedure then standard in Fascist Italy, were made to drink large quantities of castor oil and were then tied together and marched out of town. The police chief and deputy sheriff in charge of this caper were ultimately convicted in federal court of depriving the Witnesses of their constitutional rights—both men were fined and the deputy sheriff went to federal prison. But they had merely gone too far and done so too openly. In many places, the police aided the mobs by arresting their victims for "riotous conspiracy" or some similar offense, and many were given stiff fines and/or jail sentences; and sometimes, during their trials, their attorneys were beaten by mobs whom the police did nothing to restrain.

The direct result of the Gobitis decision was the wholesale expulsion of Witness children from public schools all over the United States. This took place in at least thirty-one states and possibly in all forty-eight, although in many states there were but a handful of Witness children. Some states even passed new, stronger laws requiring all school children to participate actively in the flag salute ceremony. Finally, attempts were made to take expelled Witness children away from their parents under truancy statutes and to prosecute their parents for contributing to the delinquency of minors.

Judges, especially appellate court judges and most particularly Justices of the United States Supreme Court, are often presumed to dwell in ivory towers, isolated from and oblivious to the practical effects of their theoretical decisions. But news of the frightful aftermath of the Gobitis decision penetrated even into the sacred precincts of that imposing marble building just east of the Capitol. That the public apparently deemed the Gobitis decision a hunting license for Witnesses gave many of the Justices second thoughts as to the wisdom of what they had done. Of course the Court had intended nothing of the sort, but if its decision were susceptible of such an interpretation, perhaps its decision was wrong.

Meanwhile, two more Witness cases reached the Court. They lost both of them, too.

A New Hampshire statute prohibited "parades" without a license from the affected town. A group of Witnesses marched through Manchester, a populous New Hampshire city an hour's drive from Boston, to publicize a rally at which, it was promised, religions other than Jehovah's Witnesses would be exposed as snares and rackets. The Witnesses were arrested and convicted for parading without a license. They appealed on the grounds that the statute as applied to them infringed their First Amendment rights of free speech and assembly and free exercise of religion, as well as their rights to due process and equal protection under the Fourteenth Amendment.

The Supreme Court bought none of it. The Witnesses' conviction was unanimously affirmed. Chief Justice Hughes wrote:

> Civil liberties, as guaranteed by the Constitution, imply the existence of an organized society maintaining public order without which liberty itself would be lost in the excesses of unrestrained abuses. The authority of a municipality to impose regulations in order to assure the safety and convenience of the people in the use of public highways has never been regarded as inconsistent with civil liberties but rather as one of the means of safeguarding the good order upon which they ultimately depend.

The other case which the Witnesses lost involved ordinances in Alabama, Arkansas, and Arizona which required that anyone wishing to sell books on the public streets must first obtain a license and pay a license tax. These ordinances seemed clearly unconstitutional on free speech and press grounds, according to recent rulings of the Court. But now the Court affirmed the convictions of Witnesses convicted under these ordinances who had proceeded in their usual way without benefit of licenses. Justice Reed, writing for the Court, declared: "The First Amendment does not require a subsidy in the form of fiscal exemption."

But this time the Witnesses lost by only one vote. The new Chief Justice, Harlan Fiske Stone (the lone dissenter in the Gobitis case), and Justices Black, Douglas, and Murphy dissented. In their opinion the fact that all peddlers were covered by these ordinances, while in the former cases only peddlers of books had been affected, was a distinction without a difference. Then Justices Black, Douglas, and Murphy took the extraordinary, unprecedented step of referring to the Gobitis case, which had nothing whatever to do with the case at bar, and declaring that they were sorry they had concurred in that decision. "We now believe that it was wrongly decided."

Justice Frankfurter was wild with rage. Armed with a formidable intellect and fresh from his professorship at Harvard Law School, where he had dominated his colleagues as well as his students, Frankfurter had fully expected similarly to overwhelm the Supreme Court with his brilliance. In the words of a recent biographer, "He was convinced that he held the doctrinal key to the legal universe; he was supremely confident of his ability to get on with and influence his colleagues."

Frankfurter had dominated the Court in the Gobitis case and his opinion in that case meant a great deal to him. Like the religious convert, the naturalized Frankfurter was more patriotic than many native-born Americans, and his feelings of love for this country and of gratitude for the opportunities it had afforded him were enhanced by his knowledge that in the land of his birth he would be an inmate of a concentration camp. At the same time, Frankfurter was without religious faith—he was a Jew only by reason of ancestry. "As one who has no ties with any formal religion," he said, "perhaps the feelings that underlie religious forms for me run into intensification of my feelings about American citizenship." The image of American school children refusing to pledge allegiance to the American flag, for whatever reason, filled him with revulsion.

But most of all, Frankfurter was outraged that Douglas and Murphy, both of whom had paid him fulsome compliments for his decision in the Gobitis case, should not only have changed their minds but should have announced it publicly and thereby have virtually invited an opportunity to reverse an eight-to-one decision barely two years old. As Black had joined in their announcement, and as Stone had dissented, it was obvious to all that Frankfurter's decision was now the opinion of only five members of the Court. An eight-to-one majority had dwindled to a bare single vote in record time.

Then Justice James Byrnes, who had voted against the Witnesses in all their recent cases, accepted President Roosevelt's offer to become director of the new Office of War Mobilization. As his successor the President nominated Wiley Rutledge, who as a federal appellate judge had written a dissenting opinion in which he denounced the Gobitis decision. That he would join Stone, Black, Douglas, and Murphy in forming a new majority for reversal of the Gobitis and peddlers' license cases could not be doubted.

Still, the speed with which the change took place was perhaps unseemly. *On the day Rutledge took his seat* the Court voted to grant a petition for rehearing of the peddlers' license case. That decision, not a year old, was quickly reversed. The Court was ready for a new flag salute case. It didn't have long to wait.

On January 9, 1942, at its first session after the Japanese attack on Pearl Harbor, the West Virginia Board of Education made the flag salute ceremony mandatory in all public schools in the state. Its order, which it evidently expected to be tested in the courts, tracked Frankfurter's Gobitis opinion word-for-word.

Witness children were soon expelled from public schools in every county in West Virginia. Among them were seven children living near Charleston, including two children of Walter Barnette. Barnette brought suit in the federal District Court in Charleston, asking to have the order of the Board of Education declared unconstitutional. A three-judge court was duly convened to consider the constitutional issue. The Gobitis decision was of course squarely in point and clearly required the dismissal of Barnette's suit. Nevertheless, holding that Gobitis had been "undermined" as a precedent by the dissenting opinions in the peddlers' license case, the court declared the order unconstitutional.

It was a most extraordinary decision. A lower federal court has no power to disregard a Supreme Court precedent, however "undermined" it may appear to be. The court might express the opinion that the precedent should be overruled by the Supreme Court but, until it is, it must be followed. What the court here was doing, however, was transparent. Decisions of three-judge constitutional courts may be appealed directly to the Supreme Court, bypassing the usual intermediate level of the Court of Appeals. That this case would be appealed seemed clear. The court decided to vote its conscience and leave it up to the Supreme Court to reverse if it disagreed.

In fact, the case was almost not appealed. The Attorney General of West Virginia, who expressed himself as disgusted with the whole business of trying to make devout Christian children violate their consciences, advised against an appeal; and when the Board of Education insisted, he refused to handle the case. The Assistant Attorney General was listed in the Court papers as counsel of record, but he too did not actually handle the case. That was done by retained outside counsel.

In the Supreme Court, briefs urging affirmance of the District Court's holding of unconstitutionality were filed by the ACLU and the Bill of Rights Committee of the American Bar Association, while the American Legion supported the expulsion of the Barnette children. The Board of Education's own brief relied heavily on Frankfurter's Gobitis opinion while the Witnesses, as subtle as ever, denounced the Justice as Pontius Pilate. The Court affirmed, effectively reversing Gobitis, by a vote of six to three.

Justice Black, joined by Justice Douglas, wrote, "Neither our domestic tranquillity in peace nor our material effort in war depend on compelling little children to participate in a ceremony which ends in nothing for them but a fear of spiritual condemnation." Justice Murphy wrote, "Official compulsion to affirm what is contrary to one's religious beliefs is the antithesis of freedom of worship." Justice Jackson, in an almost direct slap at Frankfurter, wrote, "To believe that patriotism will not flourish if patriotic ceremonies are voluntary and spontaneous instead of a compulsory routine is to make an unflattering estimate of the appeal of our institutions to free minds." Chief Justice Stone did not write any opinion. He was content to rest on his dissent in Gobitis, which in three years had become the law of the land.

Justices Roberts and Reed adhered to their votes in Gobitis and now dissented on the strength of Frankfurter's opinion in that case. But Frankfurter, who was devastated by the Court's rejection of *his* case, could not let it rest at that. He now wrote one of the most eloquent, heart-rending opinions ever written by a Supreme Court Justice. He poured into it all his anguish and outrage. But he did not thereby achieve a catharsis. Instead, he embarked upon a life-long vendetta against his colleagues who had abandoned him, shattering the customary civility of the Court and ultimately neutralizing the great influence which he expected to have, and probably would have had, on the development of American jurisprudence.

Frankfurter's relations with Black, Douglas, and Murphy, the three Justices who in their dissent in the peddlers' license case had invited the appeal in Barnette and virtually foreordained the result, deteriorated to an almost unbelievable level. "Hugo [Black]," Frankfurter wrote to his friend Judge Learned Hand years later, "is a self righteous, self-deluded part fanatic, part demagogue, who really disbelieves in law." "Bill [Douglas]," Frankfurter wrote in the same letter, "is the most cynical, shamelessly immoral character I've ever known. With him I have no more relation than the necessities of court work require. He is too unscrupulous for any avoidable entanglement." Even the law clerks of these feuding judges often ended by not speaking to each other—as happened with Alexander Bickel, who clerked for Frankfurter, and Fred Rodell, who clerked for Douglas, though both men became highly respected legal scholars and professors of constitutional law at Yale.

Of course Frankfurter's defeat was the Witnesses' great victory. Not only had they removed a serious impediment to the happiness of their children, not only had they caused the hunting licenses issued by Gobitis to be rescinded, they had established in the most dramatic way that states were now as constitutionally bound as the federal government to respect the right of every citizen to the free exercise of his religion.

CHAPTER VI

The Scope of Free Exercise

G EORGE W. BALLARD, alias Saint Germain, Jesus Christ and George Washington, was the spiritual leader of the "I Am" movement. After his death his wife and son continued his good and profitable work of faith healing. For this they were indicted for using the mails to defraud.

There are two elements to the crime of defrauding: (1) making a false statement for profit; and (2) knowing the statement was false when you made it. The government must prove both elements. Thus a person accused of defrauding may defend by showing *either* that the statement alleged to be false was in fact true *or* that when he made it he believed it to be true.

The government set out to prove that the Ballards made false statements when they claimed they could heal by faith, and that they knew the statements were false when they made them. But the District Court which heard the case felt decidedly uncomfortable in dealing with the truth or falsity of an essentially religious claim. It seemed too close to an inquisition for comfort. The judge accordingly instructed the jury that they could not consider whether the Ballards were in fact able to heal by faith, but only whether they sincerely believed they could.

The judge clearly believed he was advancing the cause of religious freedom in removing the issue of religious truth from the case. But the practical effect of his decision was to make it easier for the government to convict the Ballards and more difficult for them to defend themselves. For, in undertaking to prove that the Ballards' claims of faith healing were fraudulent, the government had taken on a virtually impossible task: to prove that the Ballards could not heal by faith, which would inevitably come down to a claim that faith healing was inherently a form of quackery. But faith healing is an important theme in the sacred scriptures of many respectable religions including the dominant American religion, Christianity. Did the government propose to put sellers of the New Testament in the dock?

The trouble was, if the government were not obliged to prove the falsity of the Ballards' claims, but only that the Ballards did not themselves believe in them, then for all practical purposes the Ballards would be obliged to prove the truth of their claims. For, as any trial lawyer knows, the only way to prove that a belief is sincerely held is to demonstrate that the thing said to be believed is worthy of belief, and the only way to prove that is to prove that it is true. And, to complicate the matter still further, if the truth or falsity of the Ballards' claims of faith healing were not in issue, they might not even be permitted, under the rules of evidence, to offer proof that they were true.

These anomalies were perceived by the Court of Appeals, which reversed the Ballards' conviction. Since the government charged them with making false statements, the court held, the government had to prove that the statements were false.

Unfortunately for the Ballards the Supreme Court agreed, albeit by a single vote, with the District Judge that courts may not inquire into the truth or falsity of religious beliefs but may only determine whether they are sincerely held. Justice Douglas, speaking for the majority and evidently under the impression that he was striking a blow for religious freedom, declared in ringing tones:

> Heresy trials are foreign to our Constitution. Men may believe what they cannot prove. They may not be put to the proof of their religious doctrines or beliefs . . . . The miracles of the New Testament,

the Divinity of Christ, life after death, the power of prayer are deep in the religious convictions of many. If one could be sent to jail because a jury in a hostile environment found those teachings false, little indeed would be left of religious freedom.

The logic of Douglas' opinion should have led him to vote to dismiss the indictment altogether, not just the half of it that would be particularly difficult for the government to prove. But Douglas did not even note, and perhaps he was unaware (he had never tried a case in court), that he was making it easier, not more difficult, for the state to silence purveyors of unpopular religious doctrines.

Justice Jackson, who had been a trial lawyer, realized precisely the practical effect of the Court's decision. He began his dissenting opinion by declaring that he would cheerfully sustain the Ballards' conviction if he could do so without creating a precedent. "I can see," he wrote, "in their teachings nothing but humbug, untainted by any trace of truth." But the United States Supreme Court cannot decide a case without setting a precedent, and Jackson believed that the principle which the Court was establishing—that the sincerity of religious teachers could be the subject of criminal sanctions—was pernicious and dangerous in the extreme.

Jackson quickly punctured the unrealistic notion that truth and sincerity can ever be separated. "As a matter of either practice or philosophy I do not see how we can separate an issue as to what is believed from considerations as to what is believable." But beyond procedure, truth and falsity in the religious sense are very different from the usual factual determinations which courts are called upon to make. Jackson quoted William James that religious belief is not a matter of fact but of certain kinds of experience—"conversations with the unseen, voices and visions, responses to prayer, changes of heart, deliverances from fear, inflowings of help"—and said, "It seems to me an impossible task for juries to separate fancied ones from real ones, dreams from happenings, and hallucinations from true clairvoyance."

"And then," Jackson continued, "I do not know what degree of skepticism or disbelief in a religious representation amounts to actionable fraud." Even orthodox religious teachers, he noted, "are sometimes accused of taking their orthodoxy with a grain of salt."

It is in any event difficult or impossible to assess the factual basis of religious belief, for "All schools of religious thought make enormous assumptions, generally on the basis of revelations authenticated by some sign or miracle." Finally, Jackson concluded, people do not turn to religious teachers for instruction in matters of provable fact, but for "higher values," for "truth and beauty and moral support," and who can say where or when they have found what they sought?

> There appear to be persons—let us hope not many—who find refreshment and courage in the teachings of the "I Am" cult. If the members of the sect get comfort from the celestial guidance of their "Saint Germain," however doubtful it seems to me, it is hard to say that they do not get what they pay for. Scores of sects flourish in this country by teaching what to me are queer notions. It is plain that there is wide variety in American religious taste. The Ballards are not alone in catering to it with a pretty dubious product.

But dubious as it might be, Jackson would not seek to ban it. "The price of freedom of religion or of speech or of the press is that we must put up with, and even pay for, a good deal of rubbish," Jackson declared. "I would dismiss the indictment and have done with this business of judicially examining other people's faith."

But Jackson was in a minority. A majority of the Justices of the Supreme Court seemed prepared to vote, almost blindly, in favor of any claim of free exercise—even where, as in the Ballard case, the defendants had their religious freedoms actually curtailed as a result. In fact, the Ballards might have done better to rely on their freedoms of speech and press, as a case decided by the Court a year later suggested.

A Texas statute required the registration of all union organizers operating in the state. A national labor leader came to Houston to address a mass meeting called in support of an organizational drive for an NLRB-ordered representational election at an industrial plant. Six hours before he was scheduled to speak, the labor leader was served with a restraining order issued *ex parte* (that is, without notice to him or opportunity to oppose) which prohibited him from soliciting union memberships in Texas without first obtaining an organizer's card. He did not seek to obtain a card—there was hardly time for that—and addressed the meeting anyway. He was promptly arrested for contempt of the restraining order and was convicted. The Supreme Court of Texas upheld the registration statute, which certainly seemed a transparent attempt to hinder union-organizing activities, as a necessary protection for workers against "imposters."

The Supreme Court reversed, although again by a five-to-four vote. It held that "the indispensable democratic freedoms secured by the First Amendment" were "not peculiar to religious activity and institutions alone. The First Amendment gives freedom of mind the same security as freedom of conscience. Great secular causes, with small ones, are guarded." But that being the case, the Ballards should have had the right, under the free speech and press guarantees, to profess the ability to heal by faith, and did not need the free exercise clause, which in the event proved inadequate for them, at all.

Mr. Girouard, however, seemed to need it very much indeed. He wanted to become an American citizen but when he signed the oath to support and defend the Constitution of the United States he stated that, as a Seventh Day Adventist who conscientiously objected to all warfare, he would only be willing to do so by peaceful means. That automatically disqualified him for naturalization, as the Schwimmer case demonstrated beyond question.

In 1929, the Supreme Court had rejected the plea of Rosika Schwimmer, a famous pacifist then fifty-two years old, to become a naturalized citizen because, when she was asked, "If necessary, are you willing to take up arms in defense of this country," she answered, "I will not take up arms personally." Justice Holmes, in a dissenting opinion joined by Justice Brandeis, observed that Schwimmer "seems to be a woman of superior character and intelligence, obviously more than ordinarily desirable as a citizen of the United States," and that, as a woman and over fifty years of age, she "would not be allowed to bear arms if she wanted to." Nevertheless the Court held that her opposition to war disqualified her from becoming a naturalized citizen as it rendered her unable to take without reservation the oath prescribed by Congress.

The Schwimmer case was widely criticized. Two days after the Court's decision was handed down a bill was introduced in Congress to permit the naturalization of pacifists, but it was never reported out of the House Committee on Immigration and Natural-ization. Repeated attempts over the next decade to permit a qua-lified oath were similarly blocked; and when in 1940, with Europe already at war, Congress passed a new Naturalization Act, the oath which had barred Schwimmer remained intact.

It seemed clear, then, that Girouard's application had to be de-nied. But, by a vote of five to three (Justice Jackson was in Nurem-berg as chief American prosecutor at the Nazi war-crimes trials), the Court ordered him admitted to citizenship. Surprisingly, though, the Court did not base its decision on the free exercise clause. Instead, Justice Douglas, writing for the majority, cited the prohibition contained in the body of the Constitution of religious tests for public office, and concluded, "It is hard to believe that one need foresake his religious scruples to become a citizen but not to sit in the high councils of state."

It should not have been at all hard to believe. It was a simple fact that the Constitution forbade religious tests for public office but gave Congress the power to determine whether to admit foreign-born persons to citizenship and, if it decided to admit them, to prescribe the requirements for naturalization. Moreover, the Court had frequently and consistently held that the exemption from mili-tary service of persons with conscientious objections to violence was not constitutionally required but merely a matter of legislative grace. Should it be hard to believe that Congress might refuse to admit to citizenship persons unwilling to accept military service when, if they were already citizens, they could be put in jail for refusing to accept military service?

In the Girouard case, the Court baldly added to the Naturaliza-tion Act an amendment that Congress had repeatedly considered and refused to pass. In doing so, though in terms of the prohibition of religious tests for public office, the Court had in effect extended the free exercise clause to new lengths. The way was thus paved to extend it beyond the reach of the free speech and press clauses—for the benefit, as we shall soon see, of some pretty shady charac-ters.

But first the Court turned, for the first time, to the establishment clause.

CHAPTER VII

Judicial Nonsense

ARCH R. EVERSON was the secretary of the Taxpayers' League of Ewing Township, New Jersey, through whose woods and fields George Washington's army had marched en route to Trenton. World War II was raging at its fiercest, but Everson and his friends were distracted from the war effort by their concern that, under a state statute authorizing school boards to defray the transportation costs of all school children within their jurisdictions, Catholic parochial school children would have their fares paid.

In the Supreme Court, Everson argued that, to the extent its benefits flowed to parochial school children, the statute constituted an establishment of religion. There was no suggestion, be it noted, that any one religion was being preferred over any other. The fare reimbursement plan was apparently available to all school children, public, parochial, and private secular alike. Claims under the establishment clause normally charge some governmental authority with playing favorites among religions—many scholars believe that that is precisely the meaning of establishment as used in the First Amendment. But Everson opposed any public benefit to religion *no matter how nondiscriminatory.*

That was a very extreme interpretation of the establishment clause. Indeed, to deny the benefits of a publicly financed program to specified groups solely on the basis of their religious orientation would seem to be just what the religion clauses of the First Amendment were designed to *prevent*. But before that issue could even be addressed in the Everson case, the Court had to extend the establishment clause to the states, which in 1947, when the Everson case reached the Supreme Court, had never been done.

Perhaps, applying the Court's test for extending provisions of the Bill of Rights to the states, the right to the free exercise of one's religion is "a fundamental principle of liberty and justice which inheres in the very idea of free government and is the inalienable right of a citizen of such a government." That is, apart from the history of the Fourteenth Amendment, which showed that it had not been intended to extend the free exercise clause to the states, many people might readily agree that no government, federal, state, or local, should be allowed to interfere with how a person worships. Most Americans, whatever their constitutional perspective, would be shocked if any governmental authority in America purported to forbid, upon pain of imprisonment, the celebration of the Mass or Simchat Torah. Moreover, while there are established churches in many countries where the rights of the individual are respected, no country we would consider civilized orders Christians to stay home from church or closes synagogues or mosques.

There are thus good reasons for treating the establishment clause differently from those provisions of the Bill of Rights, including the free exercise clause of the First Amendment, which had been made applicable to the states via the due process clause of the Fourteenth Amendment. At least, whether it should be treated the same or differently was the threshold issue before the Court. But the opinion for the majority was written by Justice Hugo Black, who for years had been pressing the Court to incorporate into the due process clause of the Fourteenth Amendment the entire Bill of Rights and thereby make every clause in it fully applicable to the states. It was therefore no surprise that, after referring to the cases which had incorporated other provisions of the Bill of Rights, Black simply declared, "There is every reason to give the same application and broad interpretation to the 'establishment of religion' clause."

But extending the reach of the establishment clause to the states was only half the job. Now Black had to extend the meaning of the establishment clause beyond its traditional import of playing favorites among religions. He went on:

> The 'establishment of religion' clause of the First Amendment means at least this: Neither a state nor the Federal Government can set up a church. Neither can pass laws which aid one religion, *aid all religions,* or prefer one religion over another.

The italicized phrase, slipped by Black into the middle of an otherwise unexceptional definition of establishment, may qualify as the most momentous three-word phrase in judicial history. It is on the basis of these three little words, unsupported by judicial precedent or history, that the Court has sought to destroy the financial underpinning of religious education in America while excising all reference to God from the public schools.

After all that, one would naturally expect the Court to strike down the New Jersey fare reimbursement plan as unconstitutional. But Black, reminding Justice Jackson of "Julia who, according to Byron's reports, "whispering 'I will ne'er consent,'—consented," did precisely the opposite. It was to be another example of the time-tested judicial technique of assuming a new, far-reaching power while declining to exercise it, so as to neutralize opposition to the assumption of power.

Black's ploy was successful. His four concurring brethren liked the result and the four dissenters not only wanted to extend the establishment clause to the states but wanted to use it in this case to void the New Jersey statute. No Justice was in a position to protest Black's coup.

Indeed, Justice Rutledge, writing for the dissenting minority of four Justices, stated the strict separationist position in terms so broad as to approach self-caricature. The word "religion," Rutledge wrote, means precisely the same thing in the establishment clause as it does in the free exercise clause, as proved by the word "thereof": "Congress shall make no law respecting an establishment of religion or prohibiting the free exercise *thereof.*" Accordingly, Rutledge concluded, as establishment and free exercise are but two sides of the same coin, anything protected as free exercise cannot, by reason of the establishment clause, receive any public support.

The danger of the Court's overextension of the free exercise clause was now becoming apparent—and the Court had only just begun its work in that respect. For while it may be possible to accept a very wide interpretation of free exercise as an expansion of freedom, if government support of or even association with any subject subsumed under the rubric free exercise is to be ruled out under the establishment clause, then every extension of the free exercise clause may paradoxically result in a narrowing rather than a broadening of personal freedom. It may be desirable to expand the scope of free exercise to virtually all conscientiously held beliefs, but the extension of free exercise status and protection to the great body of non-theological literature and art will be a cruel joke if as a consequence it is all placed on the establishment index.

Almost the only justification for extending the establishment clause to the states is that the Court had finally been persuaded by Justice Black that the entire Bill of Rights had to be so extended, and that to make any exception to total incorporation was to muddy the constitutional waters. But in fact the Court was not at all ready for total incorporation, despite appearances to the contrary in the Everson case, for only a few months later it again held that the Fifth Amendment privilege against self-incrimination, which some people might think closer to the core meaning of freedom than the right to make Catholic kids pay their own bus fares, was not applicable to the states. Indeed, Justice Frankfurter, whose dissenting opinion in Everson had *assumed* the incorporation of the establishment clause into the Fourteenth Amendment, now wrote an opinion in which he ridiculed the very idea of incorporation.

For seventy years after the adoption of the Fourteenth Amendment, Frankfurter wrote, forty-three Justices, including "those whose services in the cause of human rights and the spirit of freedom are the most conspicuous in our history," passed on its scope and "only one, who may respectfully be called an eccentric exception, ever indicated the belief that the Fourteenth Amendment was a shorthand summary of the [Bill of Rights] and that due process incorporated [it] as restrictions upon the powers of the states." Moreover, Frankfurter observed, if some of the provisions of the

Bill of Rights are to be made applicable to the states and some are not, how can we tell which is which? "Some are in and some are out, but we are left in the dark as to which are in and which are out. Nor are we given the calculus for determining which go in and which stay out."

Frankfurter considered his opinion in this case a great one and sent copies to his friends, one of whom congratulated him for his "devastating attack on Blackism." Certainly few stronger denunciations of Black's incorporation doctrine have been included in a Supreme Court opinion. But how could Frankfurter reconcile this opinion with the position he took in Everson that the Fourteenth Amendment made applicable to state action a clause in the First Amendment expressly limited to federal action and which, in view of our history and the contemporary reality in many other free countries, hardly qualified as one of the inalienable rights of man? Perhaps, as Emerson said, "consistency is the hobgoblin of little minds," but surely one might expect a bit more of it in a Supreme Court Justice and former law professor?

Black's incorporation doctrine, one of the most influential doctrines in American constitutional history, has been subjected to a great deal of scholarly criticism, almost all of it negative. One scholar, after reviewing the background of the Fourteenth Amendment, concluded, "In his contention that [the Fourteenth Amendment] was intended and understood to impose [the Bill of Rights] upon the states, the record of history is overwhelmingly against him." Another scholar, after reviewing the cases in detail, found that there was no more judicial than historical support for Black's position, which he characterized "as nothing more than a bald attempt to amend the Constitution by judicial fiat."

The attempt was eminently successful. The result of Black's amendment was that the establishment clause became ever more voracious until it threatened to swallow up the free exercise clause, thereby turning the original design on its head—from which undignified position, said Catholic theologian John Courtney Murray, "it cannot but gurgle judicial nonsense."

The Court had completed the federal takeover of religion in America. We shall now see what it did with its new power.

CHAPTER VIII

Released Time

WHEN KING AHASUERUS ruled the world from India to Ethiopia, the great monarch liked to display, in the words of the Book of Esther, "the wealth of his kingdom and splendor of his majesty" and as well the beauty of his wife Vashti. At the culmination of a seven-day stag party, when the king was "merry with wine," he ordered Queen Vashti to dance for his friends. She refused and he "grew hot with anger."

Ahasuerus consulted his advisers "versed in misdemeanors." They warned him that he must banish Vashti forthwith lest her act of *lèse majesté* become known and wives throughout the land be emboldened to treat their husbands with contempt. Vashti was duly banished "in order that each man might be master in his own house and control all his own womenfolk."

Though she came to an unhappy end, Queen Vashti might reasonably be thought of as, in the words of Mrs. McCollum who named her daughter after the ancient queen, "the first exponent of women's rights."

As a child Vashti McCollum attended a smorgasbord of Sunday schools and later insisted that there was no hostility to religion in her home. Indeed, she wrote in her memoirs, her mother was somewhat religious and an aunt who lived with them was very much so. She did admit, though, that her father, at all times a freethinker, did become increasingly opposed to all forms of religious expression. In 1940, Mr. McCollum expressed his opposition in a book entitled *Rationalism vs. Religious Education in the Public Schools,* the first sentence of which was: "Religious worship is a chronic disease of the imagination contracted in childhood."

In the same year that Mr. McCollum published his tract in opposition to the intrusion of religion into the public schools, the Champaign Council on Religious Education was formed to provide religious instruction in the public schools of Champaign, Illinois, where his daughter Vashti lived with her husband and their son Terry, then entering the first grade. The Council was made up of Protestant, Catholic, and Jewish parents who wished to use school time to afford their children the religious instruction they were apparently unwilling to receive after school or on weekends. In keeping with the "released time" concept then in use by some two million children in communities across the United States, the Champaign parents asked their Board of Education to permit teachers hired and paid by the Council to give a half hour per week of religious instruction to those children whose parents formally requested such instruction. The children would be released from their regular classes for this period to go to separate classrooms for instruction in the religion of their expressed preference, while children whose parents did not request religious instruction would continue with their secular studies. The Board agreed.

As religious instruction under the Champaign plan did not begin until the fourth grade, Terry McCollum was not eligible to receive it until 1943. Terry's parents did not request that he participate, but he wanted to. For one thing, he heard that the clergyman who taught the Protestant class (the McCollums had expressed no religious "preference," but as they clearly were neither Catholic nor Jewish, they were deemed Protestant by default) had been a missionary in China and brought fascinating pictures and souvenirs to class. For another thing, Terry was one of only a few children who did not attend religious class, and while the participating children heard Marco Polo stories and handled coolie hats and chopsticks, the abstainers were left to twiddle their thumbs. Terry begged his parents to sign the permission slip but they continued to refuse.

The children who took religious instruction were assessed twenty-five cents for supplies. So eager was Terry to attend that he saved up a quarter from his allowance. But just when he reached his goal his father persuaded him to spend the money on a movie. This struck Vashti as unfair. She relented and gave Terry a quarter and a permission slip.

Terry loved the religious class and was strongly affected by it. It was not a dispassionate discussion of religious concepts, be it noted, but precisely the sort of conducted religious experience normally associated with a church. "The children made posters of the Resurrection," Vashti remembered some years later, and Terry "sat and gazed at his worshipfully. This bothered me." Vashti was sufficiently bothered by the success of the religion classes that when Terry entered the fifth grade she adamantly refused to renew his permission to attend them.

The school now waged a campaign against ten-year-old Terry which made a mockery of its later claim that the released time program was voluntary. One day, for example, while the religion classes were in operation, Terry was made to sit alone in a small anteroom outside the teachers' toilet, where teachers coming and going made manifest their disapproval. Another day, he was put out in the corridor where everyone would assume he was being punished for some misconduct. When Vashti complained, Terry's teacher replied that he was not getting along well in the school because "he's the only one who doesn't take religious instruction, and that segregates him from the others. It would help if he took the course too."

Vashti sued.

Precedent was squarely against her. When Mrs. McCollum brought her suit, in 1944, the Court had not yet extended the establishment clause to the states. It had recently, in the Cantwell case in 1940, incorporated the free exercise clause into the Fourteenth Amendment, but it had never held that nonbelievers were protected under that clause. At the outset, then, she had to avoid a summary dismissal on the ground that there was no constitutional provision under which relief could be granted.

Then there was the twenty-year-old Oregon case in which the Court had held that parents had a constitutional right to send their children to private schools, including schools run by a church. If the Constitution required that a child be released from public school entirely to attend a church school, how could it be argued that the same Constitution forbade his release for a half hour of religious instruction a week?

Perhaps the most adverse precedent was the second Witness flag salute case, which the Court had just decided. It was McCollum's strongest argument that the released time program in the Champaign schools was not really voluntary, despite the school board's insistence that it was, for there were subtle pressures, and some not so subtle, on every student to participate. Thus the state was using public funds and its compulsory education law to compel children to worship, surely a violation of the establishment clause and perhaps of the free exercise clause also.

But the argument of subtle or even overt pressure seemed untenable in light of the Witness flag salute cases. While the Court had just overruled its prior decision and now held that Witness children could not be compelled against their religious scruples to salute the American flag, it had not held or even suggested that therefore, to avoid possible pressure on the Witness children to violate their consciences, nobody could salute the flag. Yet the pressures on children daily to salute the flag, especially in wartime, might be expected to be far fiercer than the pressures to participate once a week in a program of religious instruction.

Yet Vashti McCollum was not daunted by these legal difficulties any more than she was intimidated by the full-blown campaign of harassment directed against her and her family from the time her suit was filed in 1944 until it was finally decided by the Supreme Court four years later. She did not let her Biblical namesake down; and the modern Vashti won in the end.

The Supreme Court held the Champaign released time program unconstitutional by a vote of eight to one. Justice Black, who exactly one year before had written the opinion in the Everson case which extended the establishment clause to the states, again dealt with the essential issues and inconvenient precedents by ignoring them all, even the Oregon case which had established the right of parents to take their children out of the public schools altogether for education in parochial schools. Black wrote:

> Pupils compelled by law to go to school for secular education are released in part from their legal duty upon the condition that they attend the religious classes. [This] falls squarely under the ban of the First Amendment (made applicable to the States by the Fourteenth) as we interpreted it in Everson.

Justice Frankfurter, who had been passionately opposed to allowing Witness children to abstain from saluting the flag while everyone else pledged allegiance, now wrote with equal passion that Terry McCollum must not only be allowed to abstain from attending religious instruction, but that, because he wished to abstain, everyone else must be required to abstain lest Terry be pressured into participating. Ironically, Justice Frankfurter was most concerned with the divisive effects of allowing any form of religious activity in the public schools, for there now ensued a battle royal over the meaning and scope of the Court's decision. In school districts across the country parents and teachers and school administrators wondered whether all forms of religious instruction were now illegal, and if they were, whether the ban extended to school prayers, Bible readings, Christmas and Hanukkah pageants, annual performances by the school chorus and orchestra of Handel's *Messiah* or *Judas Maccabeus,* and perhaps even the singing at assemblies of "God Bless America," Irving Berlin's new song which Kate Smith was making more popular than the "Star-Spangled Banner." In some communities, religious programs of one kind or another were stopped, in others nothing changed, but in all a discordant note of uncertainty had been sounded, for no one knew what the law was. For conscientious people in particular, that is an uncomfortable position to be in.

It was all unnecessary. Had the Court adhered to its fundamental principle of judicial restraint (of which, for an additional measure of irony, Felix Frankfurter was the leading exponent) under which cases are decided on the narrowest available grounds, it could easily have avoided rendering so far-reaching a decision. For it should have been clear that the Champaign program, as administered, was not voluntary. Pressures from fellow students are one thing, with which any student representing a minority position should expect to be faced. But official pressures are a very different thing, from which students are entitled to be protected. The open attempts by the teachers in Terry's school to compel him to take religious instruction despite his parents' known opposition rendered the program coercive as to him and, as such, patently unconstitutional.

But that did not make the concept of released time inherently improper, any more than the possibility of being beaten into a confession by the police renders all confessions invalid. The courts regularly investigate claims that a confession was not voluntarily given and will not allow it to be used unless they find that it was not the product of threats, violence, or improper pressures. Similarly, the possibility that a particular program of ostensibly voluntary religious instruction might not be truly voluntary need not invalidate all programs of religious instruction. It should be possible for a court in a particular case to determine whether a program claimed to be voluntary truly respected every student's freedom of choice and to strike down only those programs where coercive pressures were brought to bear against dissenters by the authorities or were connived in by them.

But in the McCollum case, the Court did not even consider such distinctions, preferring to issue a blanket condemnation of an activity which had been going on for many years—the released time movement antedated the First World War—and which many people seemed to like. Moreover, a strange, internally inconsistent body of law was being created, as a case decided by the Court a few weeks after McCollum nicely pointed up.

A municipal ordinance in a New York town of 25,000 people prohibited the use of sound amplification equipment in public places without the permission of the Chief of Police. A Witness evangelist received a permit to use a public address system mounted on top of his car. He proceeded to use it to harangue the people on Sunday afternoons at the town's only public park, a small park with picnic tables, a playground and wading pool for small children, and facilities for horseshoes and baseball. The sound could be heard throughout the little park and resulted in complaints from people who objected to the noise. The Chief of Police accordingly revoked the Witness' permit to use a sound amplification device—he remained free to spread the Word without it—and when he used it anyway he was arrested and convicted under the ordinance.

The Supreme Court reversed his conviction by a five-to-four vote. Writing for the majority, Justice Douglas held that "loudspeakers are today indispensable instruments of effective public speech" and that it was therefore unconstitutional to prohibit their use regardless of any public annoyance which might result.

Justice Jackson, dissenting, found the decision "a startling perversion of the Constitution" (not the sort of thing one Supreme Court Justice normally says about the handiwork of another) and noted the blatant inconsistency with McCollum. "Only weeks ago," he wrote, "we held that the Constitution prohibits a state or municipality from using tax-supported property 'to aid religious groups to spread their faith.' Today we say it compels them to let it be used for that purpose. And I cannot see how we can read the Constitution one day to forbid and the next day to compel the use of public tax-supported property to help a religious sect spread its faith."

A leading constitutional scholar, among many other observers, also perceived this inconsistency. He wrote:

> At any rate, the discrepancy between the two holdings is apparent. In one it is held that a school board may not constitutionally permit religious groups to use on an equal footing any part of a school building for the purpose of religious instruction of those who wish to receive it. By the other the public authorities are under a constitutional obligation to turn over public parks for religious propaganda to be hurled at all and sundry whether they wish to receive it or not. The Court seems to cherish a strange tenderness for outre religious manifestations which contrasts sharply with its attitude toward organized religion.

How a community was to know what was permitted and what forbidden by the Constitution in this increasingly confused area was anyone's guess. But would anyone have guessed that the religion clauses of the First Amendment could be used to force a community of concentration-camp survivors to let a loudmouthed Nazi spout his vile message day in and day out on a well-travelled street corner?

CHAPTER IX

The Religion Clauses Upside Down

"CHRIST KILLERS! All the garbage that didn't believe in Christ should have been burnt in the incinerators. It's a shame they all weren't."

It was true that Carl Kunz was an ecumenical raver who called the Pope "the anti-Christ" and Catholicism "a religion of the devil." But he was pouring out his anti-Semitic filth only a few years after the world had learned that six million Jews had been incinerated and he was standing on the corner of Columbus Circle in New York City where many survivors of the Holocaust passed by every day.

New York City had an ordinance which required a street speaker to obtain a permit. Kunz's application for a permit had been granted, but when he returned to have it renewed, the police, by now aware with whom they were dealing, refused; they did not have the manpower available to prevent Kunz from being lynched. He continued haranguing passersby anyway and was arrested, convicted, and fined ten dollars.

Kunz was evidently well-financed for he had no difficulty appealing his conviction and nominal fine all the way through the New

York court system, where it was affirmed at every level. But Kunz was an ordained Baptist minister, and the United States Supreme Court could not bear the thought of a man of God being obliged to obtain a permit from a cop merely in order to preach in public. The Court voided his conviction, holding that the ordinance under which he was prosecuted was unconstitutional under the free exercise clause because, while it empowered the Police Commissioner to grant or withhold permits, it established "no appropriate standards to guide his action."

Justice Jackson, once again the lone dissenter, denounced the "appropriate standards" requirement. "This Court," he pointed out caustically, "never has announced what those standards must be, it does not now say what they are, and it is not clear that any majority could agree on them. It seems hypercritical [sic] to strike down local laws on their faces for want of standards when we have no standards."

Jackson, fresh from the Nuremberg Trials where he was chief American prosecutor, his head filled with images of the limitless brutality which can result from unrestrained hate-mongering, was even more disturbed by the substantive effects of the Kunz decision. He noted that insulting or "fighting" words had never been constitutionally protected, for their use interferes with the freedoms of those on the receiving end and threatens civil disorder. "If the City may not stop Kunz from uttering insulting and 'fighting' words," Jackson pointed out, "neither can it stop his adversaries, and the discussion degenerates to a name-calling contest without social value and, human nature being what it is, to a fight or perhaps a riot."

Of particular significance is the fact that Jackson evidently treated the case as raising freedom of speech rather than religious freedom issues. The "fighting words" doctrine had been developed to permit, in the interests of public order, some abridgment of the constitutional guarantee of free speech, and had never been applied to the religion clauses of the First Amendment. Had Jackson's colleagues agreed that this was a free speech case, as they might have done had Kunz not been a clergyman, Kunz might well have lost. By permitting Kunz to invoke the free exercise clause, the Court extended constitutional protection to a form of speech which it had previously held to be unprotected; or, rather, as it had recognized, against which society needed protection.

Having held that the American people were obliged to be subjected to amplified evangelical harangues and to unrestrained hate-mongering, the Court now returned to the task of protecting them from prayer.

New York City's released time program was different in one respect from the Champaign, Illinois, program struck down in McCollum. In Champaign, the children were released from regular classes to receive religious instruction on school grounds from teachers hired and paid by their parents, while in New York the children were released from regular classes to receive religious instruction in churches and synagogues. The Illinois program was unconstitutional. Was the New York program, constitutionally speaking, better or worse?

Six of the theologians on the Supreme Court, led by Justice Douglas, held that the New York program was better. Douglas wrote, in words which would be quoted back to him for the rest of his life, "We are a religious people whose institutions presuppose a Supreme Being." The three dissenters, Black, Jackson, and Frankfurter, thought that McCollum had settled the issue and that there was no significant difference between the cases. "The distinction attempted," Jackson wrote, "is trivial, almost to the point of cynicism . . . . Today's judgment will be more interesting to students of psychology and of the judicial processes than to students of constitutional law."

During the Eisenhower years the Court, busy now in the civil rights field, accepted few religion cases. But three cases decided by the Court in 1961 showed that the sympathy which it could so readily muster for fringe groups and characters was still not available for adherents of the traditional religions in America.

Maryland's "blue laws" prohibited various forms of commercial activity on, in the language of the Maryland Supreme Court, "the day consecrated by the resurrection of our Saviour." Massachusetts' counterpart statute, which stemmed from Puritan days, had frequently been justified in similarly theological terms. In Maryland, the employees of a store obliged under the statute to close on Sunday objected to the curtailment of their economic freedom. In

Massachusetts, suit was brought by Orthodox Jews whose religious convictions prevented them from opening their stores on Saturday, when in any event their customers, most of whom were also Orthodox Jews, would not shop. They testified that they could not make a living staying open only five days a week.

It would seem that laws explicitly making the religious observances of one religion binding on the entire population constitute as clear a violation of the establishment clause as one is likely ever to find. When such laws operate to place a special burden on the religious practices of other religions, the free exercise clause would seem also to be violated. Surely the Orthodox Jew who is told he must observe the Christian Sabbath as well as his own, while no Christian is obliged to observe the Jewish Sabbath, is placed at a far greater economic disadvantage than the Witness who must pay a small license fee to canvass a neighborhood.

It sometimes seems as if the Supreme Court's special solicitude for Jehovah's Witnesses itself constitutes a violation of the establishment clause. Surely such solicitude was not now available to the Orthodox Jews told by the state of Massachusetts that they must not work while their Christian neighbors were supposed to be at church. The blue laws were upheld, over one dissent in the Maryland case (because only economic interests were at stake), over three in the Massachusetts case (because competing religious claims were involved).

The opinion of the Court in all three cases was written by Chief Justice Earl Warren. Warren's reputation as a great civil libertarian is surely one of the wonders of the world. He built his political career, without which he would never have had a judicial career, on "Jap-baiting": as Attorney General of California in 1942 he was primarily responsible for one of the most shameful racist events in American history, the forced evacuation from the West Coast of 120,000 persons of Japanese descent, two-thirds of whom were native-born American citizens. Warren had explained the necessity to get all "Japanese" out of California and into concentration camps in the interior of the country, though none of them had been found guilty of any disloyal act, while not disturbing persons of German or Italian descent, many of whom had only recently been marching about with Nazi and Fascist flags, on purely racial grounds.

Warren now exhibited the same sympathy with the Jews before his Court as he had shown his Japanese constituents in 1942. He began by conceding that laws requiring businesses to close on the Christian Sabbath were religious in origin. Nevertheless, over the years, he explained, the emphasis had changed from religion to relaxation. (This might well be said of many religious activities. Many synagogue services, and, I am told, church services, tend to be more social than spiritual occasions. Could a state require everyone to attend some church or synagogue on the ground that the emphasis had changed and that social interaction was good for the community?) The alleged effect of the laws on Orthodox Jews, Warren declared, were purely incidental and not to be taken seriously. "The law's effect," he said, "does not inconvenience all members of the Orthodox Jewish faith but only those who believe it necessary to work on Sunday." Finally, the suggestion that observers of other Sabbaths, like Jews and Moslems, should be exempted from Sunday-closing laws (as was done in many other states), was unacceptable because it "might cause the Sunday-observers to complain that their religions are being discriminated against."

Warren, whose ability to obtain unanimous decisions from the Court was as famous as his (belated) commitment to racial equality, could not bring all his brethren with him in these cases. Justice Brennan wrote in dissent in the Massachusetts cases that an Orthodox Jew, the sincerity of whose Sabbath-observance could not be questioned, had a constitutional right to work on Sunday lest he be given "a choice between his business and his religion." Justice Stewart also dissented in the Massachusetts cases, writing, "I think the impact of this law upon these appellants grossly violates their constitutional right to the free exercise of their religion."

Justice Douglas dissented in all three cases. In his opinion Sunday-closing laws were blatantly unconstitutional under the establishment clause. The government could not, he wrote, decree universal circumcision, give tax exemptions to parents whose children are baptized, or require a daytime fast during Ramadan. By the same token the government should not be allowed to order all persons to observe the Christian Sabbath. The vice of these laws was aggravated, moreover, when they were applied to Orthodox Jews, for it "places them at a competitive disadvantage and penalizes them for adhering to their religious beliefs."

Nevertheless the Court, which had upheld the right of a Witness to shatter the peace on a Sunday with a public address system, and of a hate-monger to call every day from a well-traveled street corner for the extermination of the Jews, held that, where state law requires it, Jews must observe the Christian Sabbath.

CHAPTER X

The End of School Prayer

ONE OF THE admitted problems with school prayers is the
danger of offending one or another religious group if a
prayer offensive to it is chosen. If the authority of Jesus Christ is
invoked the prayer must offend every Jewish child (and parent), but
if His authority is not invoked Christian children (and parents) may
be upset. The Lord's Prayer is looked upon by some as nondenominational, but there are Jews who consider it a wholly Christian
prayer (authorship is after all ascribed to Jesus, though His name
does not appear in it) and there are Catholics who do not approve
of the Protestant version of it. It is all very well to refer in general
terms to "the Bible," but there are Bibles and Bibles, and wars have
been fought over which is authoritative.

The New York Board of Regents, charged to foster the well-
being of one of the most religiously diverse student populations in
the country, endeavored to solve this problem by composing a truly
nondenominational prayer. This is what it produced:

Almighty God, we acknowledge our dependence upon Thee, and we
beg Thy blessings upon us, our parents, our teachers and our Country.

67

This little prayer was disparaged as "more doctrinally flavorless than grace before a community chest luncheon," 'a short prayer of little if any religious significance," and "such a pathetically vacuous assertion of piety as hardly to rise to the dignity of a religious exercise." Nevertheless, when the school board of New Hyde Park, an affluent Long Island suburb of New York City, adopted the Regents' Prayer, suit was immediately filed by "members of the Jewish faith, of the Society for Ethical Culture, of the Unitarian Church, and one non-believer." They claimed, as the state trial judge paraphrased their complaint, that "The saying of the prayer and the manner and setting in which it is said are contrary to the religion and religious practices of those petitioners, and their children, who are believers, and to the beliefs concerning such matters held by the petitioner, and his children, who are non-believers."

For its part, the Board of Regents conceded that its prayer, though recited in conjunction with the Pledge of Allegiance, was a religious exercise. It claimed, however, and the trial judge found, that unlike the situation in McCollum there was no element whatsoever of coercion. The Board had directed that no child was to be compelled or even encouraged to say the prayer, and there was no evidence that the New Hyde Park school had violated this order.

Thus the issue was squarely presented for the first time: Is any religious exercise in a public school, no matter how brief and voluntary, prohibited by the United States Constitution?

Judge Bernard S. Meyer, the trial judge, wrote a long and careful opinion in which he reviewed in great detail the historical background of the First and Fourteenth Amendments and the relevant case law. As for the former, he concluded "that neither the sense of the nation, the debates, nor the individual views of the framers proscribe prayer as the ceremonial opening of a school day." As for the latter, he referred to the Supreme Court decisions in the Oregon case (children must be released from public school to attend private schools even if they are run by a church), Everson (a state may reimburse all parents for school bus fares even if some of their children attend parochial schools), McCollum (religious classes on school grounds during school hours are unconstitutional), and Zorach (the New York released time case—religious classes during school hours but off school grounds are valid), and concluded that "The Zorach decision constitutes a retreat from both Everson and

McCollum. The Zorach case holds that the Constitution does not require separation in every and all respects and, as we have seen, constitutional history confirms a tradition of prayer in the schools."

As for the issue of coercion, Judge Meyer reviewed the safeguards prescribed by the Board of Regents and found them essentially adequate, although he suggested a few more for the Board's consideration. But he emphasized that he was speaking about official coercion—"overt acts of the teachers or other school authorities" — and not possible embarrassment or peer pressure. "To recognize 'subtle pressures' as compulsion under the [First] Amendment is to stray far afield from the oppressions the Amendment was designed to prevent; to raise the psychology of dissent, which produces pressure on every dissenter, to the level of governmental force; and to subordinate the spiritual needs of believers to the psychological needs of nonbelievers. The equality of treatment which the Amendment was designed to produce does not require, indeed proscribes, so doing." Had the United States Supreme Court adopted such a sensible position in the McCollum case, a generation of judicial conflict could have been avoided.

Judge Meyer found the Regents' Prayer constitutional. His decision was unanimously affirmed by the five-man Appellate Division. Thus the first six judges who heard the case all agreed that the Regents' Prayer did not violate the Constitution. Nevertheless, the plaintiffs took the case up to the New York Court of Appeals. New York's highest court, in an opinion written by the Chief Judge, held:

> Not only is this prayer not a violation of the First Amendment . . . but a holding that it is such a violation would be in defiance of all American history, and such a holding would destroy a part of the essential foundation of the American governmental structure.

A concurring judge went even further:

> It is not mere neutrality to prevent voluntary prayer to a Creator; it is an interference by the courts, contrary to the plain language of the Constitution, on the side of those who oppose religion.

The protesters got two votes in the seven-member Court of Appeals. Of the first thirteen judges who considered the constitutionality of the Regents' Prayer, then, among whom were some of the most learned appellate judges in the nation, eleven found it valid, a batting average of .846; and some of them felt strongly that any other decision would be historically wrong and itself constitutionally objectionable. None of which dissuaded six United States Supreme Court Justices from declaring the prayer an unconstitutional establishment of religion.

The land was filled with roars of incredulity and outrage. It seemed amazing to persons unversed in legal legerdemain that in 1962 it should be discovered for the first time that the First Amendment (adopted 1791), even as supposedly extended by the Fourteenth Amendment (adopted 1868), forbade something which had been going on without interruption since the colonization of the American continent. Episcopal Bishop James Pike charged that the Court had "deconsecrated the nation," Cardinal Spellman, Archbishop of New York, declared that the decision "strikes at the very heart of the Godly tradition in which America's children have for so long been raised," and Father Robert Drinan, later a well-known Congressman from Massachusetts, denounced "the alliance of Protestantism, secular humanism and Judaism which controls the public schools." Former President Hoover foresaw "a disintegration of one of the most sacred of American heritages," and former President Eisenhower said, "I always thought that this nation was essentially a religious one." A conference of one hundred and twenty Episcopal clergymen agreed that "The ultimate effect of this decision may be to nullify and threaten with destruction the American people's long-continued and precious tradition of reliance upon Divine Providence." A conference of governors, by a vote of 49 to 0 (Governor Rockefeller of New York, the state involved in the case, abstained) endorsed a constitutional amendment to overturn the decision. And in Los Angeles a municipal court judge began to open her court each day with the prayer, "God bless the Supreme Court and in Your wisdom let it be shown the error of its ways."

Was the uproar justified? Had the Supreme Court really outlawed all forms of religious expression in the public schools, as its critics charged? One professor of journalism chided the press for giving that impression and for failing to note that the Court had only banned officially composed prayers. This reading of the Regents' Prayer decision seemed supported by Justice Black's opinion for the majority, in which he stated:

> We think that the constitutional prohibition against laws respecting an establishment of religion must at least mean that in this country it is no part of the business of government to compose official prayers for any group of the American people to recite as part of a religious program carried on by government.

But Leo Pfeffer, the General Counsel of the American Jewish Congress and one of the leading constitutional lawyers in America, disagreed that official composition was a limiting factor. In his opinion, "this decision makes it clear that all religious practices in the public schools, such as Bible reading, prayer recitation and religious holiday observances, are unconstitutional."

Who was correct would be known within a year. Meanwhile, it should be acknowledged that the Court's Regents' Prayer decision was the most popular it had ever rendered: in addition to the thousands of copies regularly distributed to libraries and law firms, the Government Printing Office sold 13,500 copies of it, an all-time judicial best-seller.

In a Whitestone, New York public school the kindergarten children were accustomed to saying, before they had their milk and cookies each morning, "God is great, God is good, and we thank Him for our food. Amen." After the Supreme Court ruled the Regents' Prayer unconstitutional, the education authorities in New York banned all prayers in the public schools and the principal of the Whitestone school ordered his kindergarten teachers to stop the children from saying their little prayer. A group of parents brought suit in federal court to compel the principal to rescind his order. The District Court found for the parents and told the principal to let the children say their prayer. But the United States Court of Appeals for the Second Circuit, which includes New York, reversed. The courts may not, said the Second Circuit, interfere with the principal's running of his school. "Determination of what is to go on in public schools is primarily for the school authorities." Really, that is what the court said. The Supreme Court declined to hear the parents' appeal.

CHAPTER XI

The Triumph of Atheism

S HE CALLED HERSELF Mrs. Madalyn Murray and she named her son William J. Murray III, but though a Mr. Murray was William's father he was never Madalyn's husband and William met him only once. William refers today to "the bleak depravity of life in our home" and depicts a household that was chaotic, nasty, and brutish, the tone set by his mother's "vicious and violent temper." He recalls in horrific detail the sounds of screaming arguments which sometimes spilled over into violence, as when Madalyn tried to knife her father, William's grandfather, the only member of William's family whom he remembers fondly.

Mrs. Murray paid little attention to William or to his half-brother, also illegitimate and also named Murray, although Mr. Murray was long gone from the scene. Mrs. Murray, who rarely held a job for more than six months, devoted her formidable energies to anti-religious invective and radical politics. She hosted meetings in her home of angry people who excoriated the United States and called for a dictatorship of the proletariat.

In 1959, Mrs. Murray applied to the Soviet embassy in Washington for Soviet citizenship. She pursued her application for a year without success and then, after writing to the State Department renouncing her American citizenship, took her children to Paris and haunted the Soviet embassy there for a month until she was told that she had little chance of being accepted in Russia.

Mrs. Murray thought she had wasted her time and money in France, but the Lord moves in mysterious ways. On their return to Baltimore, Mrs. Murray took William to their local public junior high school to late-register him for the ninth grade. While there she saw a class of students reciting the Pledge of Allegiance and another class saying the Lord's Prayer. She was stunned and exhilarated. She ordered William to keep notes during the school day on anything which looked like religion. This did not appeal to William, who did not like the idea of becoming the focus of trouble, and he said so. His mother responded by slapping him hard in the face and saying, "Listen, kid, the United States of America is nothing more than a fascist slave camp run by a handful of Jew bankers in New York City." She then blamed the CIA for preventing her from defecting to Russia. "Well, if they'll keep us from going to Russia where there is some freedom, we'll just have to change America. I'll make sure you never say another prayer in that school."

William kept a log, but all there was to record in it was that at the start of each day his class heard two or three verses from the Bible and then recited the Lord's Prayer and the Pledge of Allegiance. Mrs. Murray was sorry there were no further religious exercises, but these would have to do. She also read William's textbooks and found references to religion. She reported these things to the Soviet embassy in Washington and told William's school that he must be excused from the room during the morning exercises.

For more than half a century, the public school children of Baltimore had opened their school day by hearing two or three verses from the Bible, saying the Lord's Prayer, and reciting the Pledge of Allegiance—which, since 1954, included the words "under God." This was in compliance with a rule adopted in 1905 by the Baltimore Board of Education, pursuant to the authority vested in it by state statute, requiring each public school within its jurisdiction to open each school day with exercises consisting primarily of the "reading, without comment, of a chapter in the Holy Bible and/or the use of the Lord's Prayer." The Baltimore school authorities now informed the Murrays that all students must participate in the morning exercises.

Mrs. Murray kept William home from school. The authorities warned William and his mother that he was truant, but took no further action. Disappointed, Mrs. Murray wrote a letter to the Baltimore Sun. They didn't print it, but sent a reporter and a photographer to her home. Mrs. Murray was ecstatic. William: "At last Madalyn Murray had found her cause, one that would be noticed."

On October 27, 1960, the Sun published a piece on the Murrays on the first page of its local news section. Next morning, Mrs. Murray received a telephone call from a representative of the ACLU who said they were entering the case. He advised her to send William back to school, which she did. His return was a media event, but in school he was taunted as a Communist and was beaten up in the playground. The school tried to defuse the situation by having William go to the principal's office upon arrival rather than to his homeroom and thus quietly avoid the exercises, but quiet was the last thing the Murrays wanted. William sneaked into his homeroom and disrupted the Bible reading. Thereupon the Board of Education asked the state attorney general for a ruling. He replied that the exercises were constitutional, but suggested that as a matter of accommodation students who objected should be allowed to remain silent or be excused altogether.

It was a considerable victory for Mrs. Murray and in effect a complete capitulation to her demands; but she had tasted blood. William: "the whole matter was just too gratifying for Mother to give up." She got a local lawyer who was willing to work without a fee and sued in state court to stop the Bible reading and the Lord's Prayer. Her petition was denied on April 27, 1961. Next day she appealed.

Doubtless Mrs. Murray wanted to win the case, but win or lose, it had already changed her life. She was invited to become chairman of the Maryland chapter of the pro-Castro Fair Play for Cuba Committee, and eagerly accepted. She received tons of mail, many of the envelopes filled with cash or checks totalling, according to her son, "tens of thousands of dollars." Recognizing a good thing, she began systematically to solicit funds for legal expenses, and as her lawyer was not receiving a fee, she apparently made a very nice profit.

It took the Maryland Supreme Court a year to turn down the Murrays' appeal. In May 1962, they appealed to the United States Supreme Court. Meanwhile, Madalyn Murray enjoyed life more than she had ever done before. She took over a magazine called the Free Humanist, renamed it the American Atheist, and became the editor while William did the production work in the cellar of their home. She also became manager of a Communist bookstore, the New Era Book Shop, directly subsidized by the Soviet Union.

The Supreme Court heard oral argument in the Murray case together with a similar case from Pennsylvania involving a family named Schempp. The cases were almost identical, except in Pennsylvania the statute provided: "Any child shall be excused from such Bible reading, upon the written request of his parent or guardian." Thus the Schempp children needed only a note from their parents, Unitarians who disapproved of parts of the Bible, to be excused from hearing it read. But the Schempps argued that they should not be put in the position of having to single out their children for special treatment and perhaps reprisals. As they did not want their children to hear readings from the Bible, nobody should be permitted to hear them.

On June 17, 1963, the Court held eight to one that the reciting of Biblical passages in a public school was an unconstitutional establishment of religion. One hundred and fourteen pages of opinions made only one thing clear: the United States Supreme Court was as determined as Madalyn Murray to stamp out every last vestige of religion in all public schools in the country. "The result of the decision," Bishop Pike said, "is not neutrality but an imposition upon the public school system of a particular perspective on reality, namely, secularism by default, which is as much an 'ism' as any other." The Wall Street Journal was blunter: "Atheism," it editorialized, was now "the one belief to which the State's power will extend its protection."

But what about Justice Black's opinion for the Court in the Regents' Prayer case that it was the fact of official composition which constituted the constitutional offense? "It is constitutionally irrelevant," Justice Brennan now wrote in a concurring opinion, "that the State has not composed the material for the inspirational exercises presently involved." It had taken one year for Black's constitutional *test* to become constitutionally *irrelevant.* And to think the law was once thought of as slow moving!

Mrs. Murray lived off her case for years. At one point in 1976 she was earning $10,000 a week "debating" religion with a minister—they travelled around the country and gave their performance in the manner of a peripatetic circus. She channeled this money and virtually everything else she received through her nonprofit Society of Separationists and never paid any income taxes. Her home was owned by the Society as was her Cadillac.

But the case was no golden goose for William, the supposed beneficiary of the Court's solicitude for dissenters. He grew from a very unhappy boy into a very unhappy man, an alcoholic who beat his wife while she was pregnant and then abandoned her and their child, travelled around the country with a married woman, married again and again beat his wife and abandoned her and their small child, became involved in drugs and other illegal transactions, was twice arrested for assaulting police officers, was for years a fugitive from justice, and was a deserter from the Army. Today he conducts a ministry directed primarily at atheists. On May 10, 1980, the Baltimore Sun printed a letter from William Murray apologizing for his role in removing the Bible from the city's, and the country's, public schools.

(The background material in this chapter is derived from a book published in 1982 by one of the principals, William Murray. The author has no personal knowledge of Mr. Murray or his mother and has been obliged to rely upon Mr. Murray's memory and veracity.)

CHAPTER XII

The Court Steps Back

I N 1965 N E W Y O R K amended its Education Law. Previously, public school boards had been authorized to provide textbooks to public school students. Now the boards were required to loan them on a nondiscriminatory basis to all students, public and private, within their jurisdictions. A public school board, objecting that the new plan, to the extent it benefited parochial school students, was unconstitutional, sued.

Precedent was squarely in the new law's favor. In 1930, the Supreme Court had upheld a virtually identical program in Louisiana. Of course it might have been argued against the binding force of that earlier case that the religion clauses of the First Amendment had not yet been extended to the states. Instead, basing its decision in part upon that precedent, the Supreme Court now upheld the New York statute.

Then the Court turned its attention to a case which presented a stunning aspect of *déjà vu*. Susan Epperson was a young teacher of tenth grade biology at Central High School in Little Rock, Arkansas, (where in 1957 nine black children had been escorted to classes by the 101st Airborne Division). At the beginning of the 1965–66 academic year she noticed that the biology textbook newly adopted by the school board contained a chapter on evolution. As she was aware that Arkansas had a law forbidding the teaching of evolution she felt presented with a dilemma: refuse to teach the chapter and be disciplined for not doing her job, or teach the chapter and go to jail. She asked the courts to resolve her dilemma by voiding the statute under the establishment clause.

The Arkansas anti-evolution statute was modeled on the Tennessee law which in 1927 led to the spectacular Scopes "monkey trial" in which the famous trial lawyer (and atheist) Clarence Darrow and the stumpwinding populist politician (and fundamentalist preacher) William Jennings Bryan entertained the nation and provided the material for a generation of dramatic reconstructions. In the forty years of its existence no one had ever been prosecuted under the Arkansas statute and anyone who knew that it was still on the books in 1965 assumed it was a dead letter, or at least a sleeping dog which no person in authority had any intention of waking up, even for purposes of euthanasia.

Ms. Epperson had awakened the dog, however, and now the courts were obliged to decide what to do with it. The state trial court held that the statute clearly established the religious beliefs of one group and was hence unconstitutional, but the Supreme Court of Arkansas reversed on the ground that "it is a valid exercise of the state's power to specify the curriculum in its public schools." The Arkansas Supreme Court dealt with the constitutional issue by ignoring it and itself raised another issue which alone should have caused it to void the statute: "The court expresses no opinion on the question whether the Act prohibits any explanation of the theory of evolution or merely prohibits teaching that the theory is true." In other words, the statute was so vague that even the highest court in the state did not know what it meant. Vagueness is a standard ground for voiding a criminal statute under the due process clauses of the Fifth and Fourteenth Amendments.

The United States Supreme Court was very annoyed at the transparent purpose of the Arkansas Supreme Court to avoid deciding what in Arkansas was evidently a controversial issue. "With all respect," wrote Justice Harlan in a concurring opinion, "that court's handling of the case savors of a studied effort to avoid coming to grips with this anachronistic statute and to 'pass the buck' to this Court. This sort of temporizing does not make for healthy operations between the state and federal judiciaries." The Arkansas statute was clearly, as the Court now unanimously held, unconstitutional under the establishment clause, and the Arkansas Supreme Court should have said so. "Fundamentalist sectarian conviction was and is the law's reason for existence," said the Court, clearly a constitutionally improper foundation for any law.

One can sympathize with the Court in being made the scapegoat in the Arkansas case. But that was an historical curiosity. Tax exemption of church property and of contributions to religious institutions was very much an issue of current import.

It is possible that no nonprofit enterprise could survive in today's economic climate without tax-exempt status—and often direct governmental grants, too. Opera companies and symphony orchestras lose money even when they play to full houses and are wholly dependent for their existence upon tax-exempt gifts and governmental subsidies; great universities would rapidly exhaust their endowments if they could not be replenished with tax-exempt gifts and bequests from alumni; and excellent charitable organizations like the Red Cross, Catholic Charities and the Federation of Jewish Philanthropies would be obliged to curtail their activities severely if contributions to them were not tax deductible.

Churches and synagogues, and the schools they operate, are at least equally dependent upon the exemption from taxes of their property and the deductibility of contributions made to them. All fifty states grant such exemptions at least to some extent and the federal government has done so since the beginning of the Republic. A court decision holding tax exemptions for religious institutions unconstitutional under the establishment clause would do for the churches of America what Henry VIII did for the monasteries of England.

And yet a tax exemption is merely a form of subsidy, and this particular subsidy had filled the treasuries of America's churches and synagogues with billions upon billions of dollars. It was probably not an exaggeration to say that every church and synagogue in America was, if not established by federal and state governments, then certainly maintained by their largesse. It is difficult to imagine how government could more effectively establish a religion than by paying for it.

It had long been wondered what the Supreme Court would do if faced with a direct constitutional attack on religious tax exemptions. In 1970, the answer was at hand. The case arose in New York, whose constitution exempted from state taxes all property owned by organizations devoted to "religious, educational or charitable purposes" and operated exclusively for such purposes and not for profit. Frederick Walz, who owned a house in the New York City borough of Richmond, objected to the tax exemption of church property which, he said, meant that his house was assessed for more taxes than it would be if churches paid their fair share.

(A brief note for readers west of the Hudson. New York City is made up of five counties, also known as boroughs. These include Manhattan, also known as New York City; Kings, also known, at least until the Dodgers left, as Brooklyn; Queens; the Bronx; and Richmond, also, indeed exclusively, known as Staten Island. Very few people outside New York City, and not so many inside, have heard that New York City has a borough called Richmond. My father was born there. Had any New Yorker asked him where he was born, he would naturally have answered, "Staten Island." But during World War II, when he was stationed at Camp Van Dorn, Mississippi, my father found it quite useful, when asked where he was from, to say, with the broadest drawl he could muster, "Richmond.")

Richmond's Mr. Walz lost in the state courts. As tax exemption of religious institutions had been going on since the beginning of time, the courts said, they could not be unconstitutional. Perhaps it should be noted that New York elects its judges.

In the United States Supreme Court, Justice Douglas, noting that "A tax exemption is a subsidy," wrote, "Direct financial aid to churches or tax exemptions to the church qua church is not, in my view, even arguably permitted." He went on:

> The religiously used real estate of the churches today constitutes a vast domain. Their assets total over $141 billion and their annual income at least $22 billion. And the extent to which they are feeding from the public trough in a variety of forms is alarming.

'I conclude," Justice Douglas wrote, "that this tax exemption is unconstitutional." But Douglas stood alone. At the brink of the abyss all eight other Justices of the Supreme Court stepped back. For, if a decision that tax exemption of church property is unconstitutional would destroy the churches, it might also end the American experiment with an independent judiciary. So Chief Justice Burger gathered his brethren around him, excepting only William Douglas, and found no constitutional objection to the pervasive system of tax exemptions for religious institutions.

The Chief Justice assigned the opinion to himself. With rare and admirable candor, Burger admitted the "considerable internal inconsistency" in prior opinions of the Court in religion cases. He stopped short of overruling those cases—for which he probably had no majority—but warned against "placing too much weight on a few words or phrases of the Court." He even noted Jackson's dissent in the Everson case where, quoting Byron, Jackson had called sarcastic attention to the discordance between the reasoning of Black's opinion for the Court, in which the establishment clause was extended to the states for the first time, and its conclusion that a state could reimburse parochial school parents for their children's school bus fares. "One can sympathize with Mr. Justice Jackson's logical analysis," the Chief Justice now wrote, "but agree with the Court's eminently sensible and realistic application of the language of the Establishment Clause."

In other words, logic be damned, we're not going to overrule tax exemptions. And they didn't. Declaring that "an unbroken practice of according the exemption to churches . . . is not something to be lightly cast aside," Burger concluded:

> Nothing in this national attitude toward religious tolerance and two centuries of uninterrupted freedom from taxation has given the remotest sign of leading to an established church or religion and on the contrary it has operated affirmatively to help guarantee the free exercise of all forms of religious belief.

Which, needless to say, but which the Court had refused so far to say, could equally be said for prayers and Bible recitation in the public schools. But Burger had only been Chief Justice for a year. The Court's next opinion in a religion case was eagerly awaited.

CHAPTER XIII

Judicial Chaos

S HORTLY AFTER THE Supreme Court approved New York's statute providing for the loan of textbooks to all students in the state, including those attending parochial schools, Rhode Island passed a statute providing salary supplements for teachers in all private elementary schools in Rhode Island, and Pennsylvania sought to provide direct subsidies of teacher's salaries and secular textbooks in all elementary and secondary schools in that state. At the time these statutes were passed, 25 percent of elementary school pupils in Rhode Island, and 20 percent of elementary and secondary school pupils in Pennsylvania, attended private schools, nearly all of them parochial schools of the Catholic Church.

The Supreme Court heard oral argument in cases attacking both of these statutes just ten months after its decision in Walz. It was widely hoped that Chief Justice Burger would render another "eminently sensible" opinion. The opinion he did render in Lemon v. Kurtzman, in which an eight-Justice majority struck down both statutes as unconstitutional establishments of religion, could not have been more disappointing. Indeed, the tripartite test which Burger now laid down for these cases became the tests which would drive everyone, including Burger, crazy for years to come. Burger wrote:

> First, the statute must have a secular legislative purpose; second, its principal or primary effect must be one that neither advances nor inhibits religion; finally, the statute must not foster an excessive government entanglement with religion.

Three criteria, *all* of which must be met before a statute can pass constitutional muster: (1) secular purpose, (2) primary effect neutral as to religion, and (3) no excessive government entanglement with religion. It is immediately obvious that tax exemption of churches fails at least the first two tests. As failure of *any* of Burger's tests was supposed to render a statute unconstitutional, the tax exemptions were evidently doubly invalid. But the Court had held them valid by an overwhelming majority. Thus the Chief Justice wrote two opinions a year apart, the first of which approved the most massive possible aid to religious institutions through total tax exemptions, and the second of which condemned programs of much less significance pursuant to tests which would have utterly invalidated the first.

Read in the light of his opinion in Walz, Burger's opinion in Lemon v. Kurtzman seems to have been written by the Mad Hatter. First the Chief Justice found that both of the statutes under review had legitimate secular purposes (to aid all education) and that a sincere attempt had been made by both the Rhode Island and Pennsylvania legislatures to avoid assisting religious activities (by expressly limiting aid to secular subjects and by prescribing auditing and reporting procedures to implement such limitations). Under the first two tests now laid down by Burger, then, the Rhode Island and Pennsylvania school aid statutes were far less offensive, from a constitutional point of view, than the church tax exemption upheld in Walz. Nevertheless, indeed *as a consequence* of the legislatures' efforts to avoid improper subvention of religious institutions, "the cumulative impact of the entire relationship arising under the statutes . . . involves excessive entanglement between government and religion."

Truly worthy of Lewis Carroll. Or perhaps Joseph Heller, for

Justice White, the lone dissenter, perceived the Catch-22 aspects of the Court's decision:

> The Court thus creates an insoluble paradox for the State and the parochial schools. The State cannot finance secular instruction if it permits religion to be taught in the same classroom; but if it exacts a promise that religion not be so taught—a promise the schools and its teachers are quite willing and on this record able to give—and enforces it, it is then entangled in the "no entanglement" aspect of the Court's Establishment Clause jurisprudence.

Not content with inconsistent decisions a year apart, the Court now proceeded to render, on the very same day the Lemon test was offered to the world, a contrary decision in an identical if not more egregious case. Under a Higher Education Facilities Act the federal government was authorized to make grants and loans to colleges throughout the country, including sectarian schools, for the construction of academic facilities. Of course the Act provided that such facilities must not be used for religious purposes, but so did the Rhode Island and Pennsylvania statutes struck down by the Court in Lemon. Nevertheless, having struck down state statutes designed to afford a small amount of relief to hard-pressed parents of parochial school children, the Court simultaneously upheld the vastly more comprehensive program of direct federal aid to sectarian colleges.

The Chief Justice had the decency to admit that "candor compels the acknowledgment that we can only dimly perceive the boundaries of permissible government activity in this sensitive area of constitutional adjudication." But legislation is not a game where you win some, you lose some. A great deal of time, money, and political capital is expended in the passage of a statute, and as it usually takes years for the Court to pass on a new law, honest people may have changed their lives in reasonable reliance on the continuance of the programs thus set in motion. To play now-you-see-it-now-you-don't with legislation is to play now-you-see-it-now-you-don't with people's lives.

And the Court continued to show a strange solicitude to fringe groups wholly at variance with its treatment of mainline religion.

Jehovah's Witnesses being in short supply for the moment, the Court turned its attention to the Amish, those quaint horse-and-buggy people who were spread through Pennsylvania and the Midwest.

Wisconsin's compulsory school-attendance law required every child in the state to attend school until the age of sixteen. They could attend a private school, secular or religious, or a public school, but they had to attend some school until the prescribed age. The Amish refused to send their children to school after the age of fourteen, preferring to put them to work on their farms and to isolate them from such corrupting influences as television, radio, telephones, automobiles, jeans, and freedom.

The Supreme Court now held, without a single dissent, that the Amish had a constitutional right to keep their children home. The Court, which had been declaring in case after case that what obtained in 1789 or 1868 need not control what should obtain today, now stated:

> We must not forget that in the Middle Ages important values of the civilization of the Western World were preserved by members of religious orders who isolated themselves from all worldly influence against great obstacles.

The comparison of Old Order Amish, who have one book in their houses, with medieval monasteries where great scholars labored for years on major works and translations, was absurd. Besides, the Court's rationale would seem to require the exemption from compulsory school-attendance laws of the children of a commune or of any parent who preferred to isolate them from the corrupting influences of basic literacy and child-labor laws. Compulsory school laws were passed precisely to prevent parents from making their children work instead of sending them to school. The Supreme Court was according to the Amish a control over their children contrary to all American tradition.

There was, had the Court not been dazzled by the conjunction of a fringe religious group and a claim under the free exercise clause, an alternative to exempting Amish children from all school requirements. The Amish could readily have set up their own high schools where state-mandated subjects could be taught by Amish teachers in an atmosphere congenial to Amish customs. It is entirely possible to study English, American history and government, algebra, and science without watching television, listening to the radio, speaking on the telephone, driving an automobile, or wearing jeans, just as it is possible to study such subjects while being immersed in Aquinas or the Talmud—as the states say children in Catholic and Jewish parochial schools must do. Indeed it would seem that a state which made Catholic and Jewish children follow a state-mandated curriculum until the age of sixteen but released Amish children at fourteen would be guilty of violating both the establishment and equal protection clauses. Yet the Supreme Court now held that a state must do just that—must make invidious comparisons among religious groups (there are Jewish sects which are just as desirous of avoiding heathen contamination as the Amish) and accord one of them privileges not available to the others, and this on constitutional grounds, though it seemed to go against everything the Constitution had always been thought to stand for.

If there was one thing the Justices of the Supreme Court could agree upon, it was that the establishment clause forbade the federal government to set up chapels and compel people to attend them. Yet that is exactly what the federal government had done in the national military academies. There was some provision for non-believers to abstain from attending services, but few cadets—none at West Point— had ever done so. For all practical purposes every cadet at West Point, Annapolis, and the Air Force Academy at Colorado Springs was obliged to go to church or synagogue every Sunday (yes, Jewish services were held on Sundays).

In 1972, the practice came for review before the United States Court of Appeals for the District of Columbia. The military authorities argued that requiring cadets to go to church every week had a purely secular purpose:

> The sole purpose of chapel attendance is to develop in the cadets, through observation of the impact of religion on the lives of others during actual worship services, that sensitivity to religious emotion which is required of a military leader.

Of course the cadets were at services to worship, not observe; and as they only attended the services of their own churches, there were no "others" to observe. Moreover, spokesmen for religious groups who testified in favor of compulsory prayers expressed shock and disgust at the suggestion that religious worship was a mere instructional aid. Anyway, the court held that the procedure was unconstitutional:

> Compulsory church attendance was one of the primary restrictions on religious freedom which the Framers of our Constitution sought to abolish.

The Supreme Court declined to hear an appeal from the decision of the Court of Appeals. Interestingly, no one took the position that, as compulsory attendance at church services was unconstitutional, no one should be allowed to attend church services on the premises of the academies, lest cadets be pressured into attending —the reasoning of the McCollum case.

New York, whose plan to loan textbooks to all students in the state on a nondiscriminatory basis had been upheld by the Court, now tried to give additional assistance to low-income families with children in parochial school. The means it chose included grants for "maintenance and repair" to non-profit private schools with high concentrations of low-income children (most of which were run by religious institutions), direct tuition reimbursement to low-income parents of children in such schools, and tax deductions for low- and middle-income parents of such children.

The Supreme Court struck the entire program down as unconstitutional under the establishment clause. Six Justices agreed that all aspects of the assistance program were unconstitutional but Chief Justice Burger and Justice Rehnquist, just appointed to the Court, believed that only the direct grants for maintenance and repair were objectionable (because they went directly to the schools) while Justice White thought the entire program was legal.

The majority decision was based squarely on the tripartite test formulated by the Chief Justice in Lemon v. Kurtzman—rather strange, since Burger was here in dissent. The majority concluded that while the statute might have the legitimate secular purpose of assisting low-income families to pay for the kind of education they wanted for their children and had a constitutional right to select for them, its primary effect was to advance religion. The program thus failed Burger's second test and thereby ran afoul of the establishment clause. It was true that the free exercise rights of poor parents who wished to send their children to parochial school might suffer as a consequence. "But this Court repeatedly has recognized that tension inevitably exists between the Free Exercise and the Establishment Clauses . . . and that it may often not be possible to promote the former without offending the latter." The Court did not endeavor to explain why in such circumstances the establishment clause should prevail over the free exercise clause.

On the same day that the Court struck down the New York plan to assist low-income families with children in parochial school, it also voided another New York statute, this one authorizing the reimbursement of private schools for the costs of preparing and administering *state-mandated* examinations. Chief Justice Burger, writing for the Court, held:

> We cannot ignore the substantial risk that these examinations, prepared by teachers under the authority of religious institutions, will be drafted with an eye, unconsciously or otherwise, to inculcate students in the religious precepts of the sponsoring church.

Well, of course. That was why children were in parochial schools in the first place—to be inculcated with the religious precepts of the sponsoring church; and the Supreme Court had said they had a constitutional right to be there. Since the statute provided no safeguards against this *danger,* Burger wrote, the statute was unconstitutional. Of course if the statute had provided such safeguards, it would have run afoul of Burger's "entanglement" test.

Pennsylvania tried again to meet the new constitutional standards being enunciated by the Supreme Court. The legislature authorized the provision to all private schools of books "which are acceptable for use in any public elementary or secondary school of the Commonwealth," "instructional materials and equipment" such as periodicals, maps, charts, photographs, records and films, and such "auxiliary services" as counseling, testing, speech and hearing therapy, remedial teaching, "and such other secular, neutral, non-ideological services as are presently or hereafter provided for public school children of the Commonwealth."

Clearly the Pennsylvania legislature was trying desperately to provide a plan which would meet the Court's establishment clause standards. But except for the books, which the Court permitted on the authority of the New York case, it struck down the entire Pennsylvania program. Justices Douglas, Brennan and Marshall would also have forbidden the books, while Chief Justice Burger and Justices White and Rehnquist would have permitted everything.

Burger, who, after all, was presiding over this disintegrating Court, was deeply disturbed over the increasingly doctrinaire and inflexible attitude his brethren were adopting (though his opinion in Lemon v. Kurtzman was responsible for much of the trouble) and, now in dissent, wrote:

> To hold, as the Court now does, that the Constitution permits the States to give special assistance to some of its children whose handicaps prevent their deriving the benefit normally anticipated from the education required to become a productive member of society and, at the same time, to deny those benefits to other children *only because* they attend a Lutheran, Catholic, or other church-sponsored school does not simply tilt the Constitution against religion; it literally turns the Religion Clauses on their heads.

Justice Rehnquist, joined by Justice White, was of a similar mind:

> I am disturbed as much by the overtones of the Court's opinion as by its actual holding. The Court apparently believes that the Establishment Clause of the First Amendment not only mandates religious neutrality on the part of government but also requires that this Court go further and throw its weight on the side of those who believe that our society as a whole should be a purely secular one. Nothing in the First Amendment or in the cases interpreting it requires such an extreme approach.

When the Court struck down New York's low-income assistance statute it did pay the legislature the compliment of recognizing that it had endeavored in good faith "to tailor state aid in a manner not incompatible with the recent decisions of this Court." The Maryland legislature also tried when it passed a statute under which private colleges in the state could receive subsidies proportional to the appropriations for public colleges. "None of the moneys payable under this subtitle," the statute carefully provided, "shall be utilized by the institutions for sectarian purposes."

It worked, but just. The Court upheld the statute five to four. Moreover, five separate opinions were rendered and the majority fobbed off the entire responsibility for the result on the three-judge District Court which had, by a two-to-one vote, upheld the statute on the grounds that the private colleges which would benefit from the statute were not "so permeated with religion that the secular side cannot be separated from the sectarian" and that the administrative safeguards against religious use were sufficient and yet not excessively entangling. Since these findings were not "clearly erroneous," the Court held that they were "binding" and hence that there was nothing left for the Supreme Court to do but apply its rubber stamp to the District Court's conclusion that the statute was constitutional. It was not an edifying performance but it was presumably the only way a bare majority could be held together.

Now the Court turned to another Witness case, more far-fetched even than the others, with predictable results. The state of New Hampshire, like many other states, liked to adorn its license plates with the mobile equivalent of grandma's samplers. New Hampshire's sampler read "Live Free or Die." George Maynard and his wife, Jehovah's Witnesses who the Court carefully informed posterity owned a Toyota Corolla and a Plymouth station wagon (it is not indicated if the case would have been decided differently had they owned a Ford or Chevrolet), put tape over the motto on their license plates because they found it to be "morally, ethically, religiously and politically abhorrent." The state of New Hampshire, whose prosecutors were evidently under-employed, brought Mr. Maynard to criminal court for defacing state property. He was tried, convicted, and jailed. ("Hey, man, what you in for?" "Well, you see . . . .")

After serving his sentence, Mr. Maynard moved in the federal courts to enjoin the state courts from prosecuting him again for an act he fully intended to repeat. An injunction was granted and the state appealed to the Supreme Court.

Chief Justice Burger delivered the opinion of the six-man majority forbidding New Hampshire from ever again infringing the Maynards' constitutional right to deface their license plates. "We are faced," he wrote, "with the question of whether the State may constitutionally require an individual to participate in the dissemination of an ideological message by displaying it on his private property in a manner and for the express purpose that it be observed and read by the public. We hold that the State may not do so."

Justice Rehnquist, in dissent, came as close as he ever did to ridiculing an opinion of the Chief Justice. Indeed, Rehnquist was joined in his opinion by Justice Blackmun, who had been best man at Burger's wedding and who was usually so closely allied to Burger that the two were called the "Minnesota twins." Rehnquist pointed out that screwing a license plate onto your car in compliance with the motor vehicle law can hardly be deemed an affirmation of belief in whatever the state has written on it. To avoid any misunderstanding, moreover, the Maynards could display a bumper sticker expressing their disagreement with the sentiments of their license plates.

Justice White also dissented, but on technical grounds. Surprisingly, though, no one cited the old legal maxim, *de minimus non curat lex* (the law does not resolve trifles). By writing serious opinions in so insignificant a case the Court only got itself into logical conundrums it would have been better advised to avoid. For example, if a license plate motto is forbidden on constitutional grounds, what about "In God We Trust" on the coinage? On the other hand, would a bumper sticker suffice to neutralize a license plate upon which the state had required "Jesus Saves" be inscribed? (What would the bumper sticker say, that He doesn't?) Justices should not be heard to complain, as some are wont to do, about their crushing workload if they have time for cases like this.

Back to the problems of education and the confused state legislatures. Ohio passed a statute which authorized the state to provide students in private schools, including parochial schools, with textbooks, instructional materials and equipment, standardized testing and scoring materials, diagnostic and therapeutic services, and transportation for field trips. Amounts supplied under these programs were limited to per pupil expenditures in the public schools.

Chief Justice Burger and Justices White and Rehnquist voted to uphold all the programs, and Justice Brennan voted against them all. The remaining Justices voted for some and against others. The diagnostic services program won 8–1, the therapeutic services program won 7–2, the textbooks and testing programs won 6–3, the field trip transportation program lost 4–5, and the instructional materials and equipment program lost 3–6.

Having caused the establishment clause to swallow up the free exercise clause, the Court now held that the free exercise clause must be deemed to have swallowed up the establishment clauses in state constitutions. As has been mentioned, many state constitutions are more strictly separationist than the federal Constitution. Thus, while under the federal Constitution any citizen who meets the age and residency requirements can serve in Congress (religious tests for federal office are expressly prohibited in the body of the Constitution), the Tennessee constitution prohibited clergymen from serving as legislators. It had so provided since 1796 when Tennessee became the third state admitted to the Union, and it had never occurred to anyone that it could not always so provide.

In the mid-1970s, Tennessee convened a constitutional convention. Delegates had to be qualified to sit in the state legislature, which effectively excluded clergymen. One such sued, and the Supreme Court held that the Tennessee constitution deprived him of his free exercise rights under the federal Constitution.

The decision called into question for the first time all the state constitutions and laws which provide a *higher* wall of separation between church and state than the federal Constitution. The ramifications of this totally unexpected development were staggering, but before they could be explored the Court held (5–4), in an even more ridiculous expansion of the free exercise clause, that teachers in church-sponsored schools were not covered by the National Labor Relations Act and hence had no protection against unfair labor practices.

The strict separationists on the Court were fond of quoting Jefferson and Madison on the meaning of the First Amendment. Both of them would have been appalled by the notion that it prevented a state from restricting the political activities of clergymen or that it gave religious institutions a constitutional right to oppress their workers.

CHAPTER XIV

Applying the Brakes

THE ERA OF judicial activism and innovation was ushered in by the social needs generated by the Great Depression. It was brought to a close on the sands of the Persian Gulf.

Some day, when the history of the United States in the twentieth century is written, the Iranian crisis of 1979–81 may well figure as one of the great watersheds, ranking with the wars and the Great Depression in its impact on the American psyche. In some ways, those 444 agonizing days may have changed the way Americans look at themselves even more than any of the other events.

We entered World War I thinking we would clean up the European mess in short order—and we did. We entered World War II realizing that it would be a long battle but assuming that we would win in the end— it was and we did. We went to Korea to save a country from Communist takeover—and we did. We failed in Vietnam but we did so voluntarily—we chose not to use all our military might, and we believed that had we used it we would have won, at least in a military sense.

But the Iranian crisis was different, a real first in American history. Every day we watched our diplomats and marines being abused and humiliated; we wondered what worse was happening to them beyond the reach of the cameras; and we seemed helpless to do anything but wring our hands and participate in a long legal farce in international tribunals which had long since ceased to have any meaning in the real world.

The Iranian hostage debacle led to a period of self-examination in the country not seen since the days of the Great Depression. While this is hardly the place even to summarize the range of diagnoses and suggestions of treatment for what was widely called our fall from grace, one theme sounded throughout like the ground bass in an organ passacaglia: we had become unserious, careless with our incomparable patrimony. We had allowed our productive capacity, once the wonder of the world, to decay to the point where many nations had surpassed us, our educational establishment to deteriorate to the point that an appallingly high proportion of our young people were functionally illiterate and unable to cope in a modern economy, and our military capacities to fall, despite the expenditure of unimaginable sums on armaments, to the point that our representatives abroad were wholly dependent upon the good will, often non-existent, of their host governments. Meanwhile, the Germans and the Japanese and even the supposedly lackadaisical French were *working* and building industrial plants with which we would find it increasingly difficult to compete. And the funny foreigners were even, unkindest cut of all, having a better time than we were in cities relatively free from crime and poverty.

These mordant observations, which were made by responsible people all across the political spectrum, lent a sense of urgency to questions which had rarely been seriously debated outside academic circles. Should we give ailing industries government support and protection against foreign competition during their period of convalescence or should we allow the marketplace to sort things out in its own inimitable way? Should our schools place increased emphasis on science and foreign languages and provide each child with a personal computer? Should our tax system be revised to encourage savings and investment? Should we build new missile systems or concentrate on our "conventional" forces?

Our courts were fully taken up by this new mood of questioning.

Had we provided so many safeguards for persons accused of crimes that our trials had become procedural mazes in which final conviction of the most egregiously antisocial person took years, years during which he was given full opportunity to prey on additional victims? Had we provided so soft a security net for persons unable to find work that they often were given greater purchasing power than the hard-working employed? Had we promulgated so many rules to limit pollution and make workplaces safer that we had priced many of our industries out of the market?

Perhaps most of all, our new awareness of our vulnerability to the ills which beset the rest of mankind made us less willing to take unnecessary chances. The days of careless experimentation with our basic social document, to which to a great extent we owed our almost unique freedoms, were drawing to a close. In the area which is the subject of this book, the result was a virtual admission by the Supreme Court that the original plan of the Constitution was wiser than anything the Court had superimposed upon it during forty years of improvisation. Beginning in 1980 the Court undertook to unravel the peculiar tapestry it had woven with threads from the First and Fourteenth Amendments and to restore, as closely as possible, the original fabric.

It was to prove a difficult task; in some respects, as where school prayers were concerned, the equivalent of unscrambling an egg.

The process began early in 1980. In 1973, as discussed in the last chapter, the Supreme Court had invalidated a New York statute which provided funds for private schools, including church-sponsored schools, to reimburse them for the costs of administering state-mandated examinations. After that decision New York passed a new statute, nearly identical with the invalidated law except that auditing procedures were prescribed to make certain that none of the funds appropriated under the act could be used for religious purposes.

Past decisions of the Court seemed to doom this new statute, for its auditing requirements only added an entanglement issue to the constitutional infirmities of the old act. But by a five-to-four vote the Court now held that the new statute was acceptable. The Chief Justice, perhaps wishing subtly to suggest that the Court had changed its mind, assigned the opinion to Justice White, the sole dissenter in the 1973 case. That the Court was overruling its prior holding *sub silentio* was all too obvious to the four protesting dissenters, who found the new statute *more* constitutionally offensive, because of the auditing requirement, than the old one.

The next religion case which reached the Supreme Court involved the celebration in the public schools of Sioux Falls, South Dakota, of Christmas and Hanukkah, and Easter and Passover. While the United States Court of Appeals for the Eighth Circuit, by a vote of two to one, held that such celebrations did not offend the Constitution, the dissenting judge thought that they could not have been more unconstitutional, for they (1) did not have a secular purpose, (2) had the principal or primary effect of advancing religion, and (3) excessively entangled the school district in religious affairs, thus failing all three of the Chief Justice's establishment clause tests. Nevertheless, on November 10, 1980 the Court declined to accept an appeal from the Eighth Circuit's decision upholding the constitutionality of these celebrations.

A week later, the Court invalidated a religious program in the Kentucky public schools. But the decision, in what a few years before would have been a clear case of a blatant violation of the establishment clause, was by a five-to-four vote.

The Kentucky statute in question required the posting of a copy of the Ten Commandments on the wall of every public school classroom in the state. Each copy was to be twenty inches high by sixteen inches wide. The statute dealt with the anticipated constitutional objection as follows:

> In small print [sic!] below the last commandment shall appear a notation concerning the purpose of the display, as follows: "The secular application of the Ten Commandments is clearly seen in its adoption as the fundamental legal code of Western Civilization and the Common Law of the United States."

The Ten Commandments do not constitute "the fundamental legal code of Western Civilization." There are no legal restrictions in any Western country on the making of carved images or the taking of the Lord's name in vain or the honoring of one's parents or the coveting (modern advertising, pervasive in every

Western country, is the art of induced coveting) of one's neigh-
bor's house, slave, slave-girl, ox or ass; and murder, theft and
adultery are proscribed in every legal code of whatever origin. As
for "the Common Law of the United States," there is no such
thing. But perhaps more offensive than its inaccuracy was the insulting legislative belief that so transparent a device would persuade any self-respecting court to uphold an otherwise patently
unconstitutional establishment of religion. The legislature was not
entirely wrong, however, for the state trial court upheld the statute precisely on the basis that its "avowed purpose" was "secular
and not religious" and the Kentucky Supreme Court affirmed, albeit by an equally divided court. Indeed, in the United States
Supreme Court, Justice Rehnquist felt bound to accept the legislature's claim of a secular purpose, and three other Justices, though
unwilling to close their eyes to reality quite so tightly, still felt
that the program was constitutionally acceptable. The Court reversed, however, and held:

> The Ten Commandments are undeniably a sacred text in the Jewish
> and Christian faiths, and no legislative recitation of a supposed sec-
> ular purpose can blind us to that fact.

During the next term of Court another Jehovah's Witness case
appeared on the docket. A Witness worked in a steel foundry in
Indiana for about a year. Then the foundry was closed and he was
transferred to a division of the company which made tank turrets.
He said that for religious reasons he could not work on weapons,
and as the company only had weapons-producing jobs available, he
asked to be laid off. The company refused and he quit. As a consequence of "voluntarily" leaving his job he was found ineligible for
state unemployment benefits. The Supreme Court held that the
finding of ineligibility was an unconstitutional deprivation of his
free exercise rights.

But a couple of months later, in a case nearly identical with the
series of cases in which the Court had invalidated ordinances seeking to restrict the canvassing activities of the Witnesses, it found in
favor of such a law. A Minnesota public corporation which conducted agricultural fairs, required all persons desiring to sell or

distribute any merchandise at the fair, including printed matter, or to solicit funds, to do so only from booths rented on a first-come-first-served basis. Violation was made a crime. This restriction on their evangelical activities was challenged in the state courts by the International Society for Krishna Consciousness. On the basis of the old Witness cases, the Minnesota courts agreed with the Society and held the rule unconstitutional. The Supreme Court reversed, holding that the booth-rental rule was reasonable and, according to the record, evenhandedly administered.

The Court still was not ready to deal with school prayers, however. When, in October 1981, a case reached it from the Ninth Circuit, where the Court of Appeals had struck down a program in an Arizona public high school in which the Student Council was allowed by the school authorities to open its assemblies with a prayer, the Supreme Court declined to consider an appeal.

At last, on December 8, 1981, the Court rendered an opinion in a school prayer case which, in the light of its prior opinions in this area, certainly seemed to indicate a new approach.

At the University of Missouri, more than a hundred student groups were officially recognized and allowed to use school facilities for their activities. One of these groups was made up of about twenty Christian students who conducted public meetings involving prayers, hymns, Bible readings, and discussions about religious subjects. Between 1973 and 1977 the university allowed this group to hold its meetings in classrooms and at the student center. Then the university decided that these meetings violated the United States Constitution and the even more strictly separationist constitution of Missouri, and barred the group from further use of university facilities.

The students sued, arguing that their exclusion from public facilities which a hundred other groups were allowed to use, solely on the basis of the religious content of their meetings, violated their constitutional rights of free exercise, free speech, and equal protection of the laws. The university officials defended on the ground that the constitutions of the United States and Missouri obliged them to deny the use of the facilities of a public university for religious purposes. The District Court, basing its decision on prior decisions of the Supreme Court, agreed with the university. The

Court of Appeals for the Eighth Circuit disagreed, holding that the university could, under the establishment clause, allow a religious group to hold meetings on university property, and therefore was obliged, by the free exercise clause, to do so on an equal basis with other groups.

The Supreme Court affirmed eight to one, holding that the establishment clause of the federal Constitution did not forbid the non-discriminatory use of public facilities by religious groups, that the free exercise clause required it, and that if the Missouri constitution forbade it, the Missouri constitution was preempted and overruled by the federal Constitution. Justice White dissented on the basis that in his opinion the federal Constitution neither required nor forbade the university to make its facilities available to any group, religious or secular. Thus, all nine Justices of the Supreme Court agreed that a public university has the right, and eight Justices held that it has the obligation, to make its facilities available to all comers on an equal basis, even though some of them might be religiously oriented and intending to hold religious meetings.

It will be remembered that in the released time case involving Vashti McCollum and her son Terry, the Court had held that religious classes on public school property were unconstitutional. Subsequent cases, in particular the Murray case in Baltimore, indicated that the constitutional infirmity was the use of public school facilities for religious exercises. Did the University of Missouri case mean that the Court had changed its mind?

On the strength of the prior cases, the United States Court of Appeals for the Second Circuit had upheld the refusal of a public school to permit students acting on their own initiative to hold prayer meetings on school property before the beginning of the school day. While agreeing with the students that their free exercise rights were being infringed, the court held that the school authorities had to deny their request, for prayers on school premises constituted *per se* (that is, regardless of the circumstances) an establishment of religion. The main problem, according to Judge Irving R. Kaufman, one of the great federal appellate judges, was that, no matter by whom initiated or how administered, school prayers could never be voluntary. "An adolescent may perceive 'voluntary' school prayer in a different light if he were to see the captain of the school's football team, the student body president, or the leading actress in a dramatic production participating in communal prayer meetings in the 'captive audience' setting of a school."

There was one significant distinction, and only one, between the Missouri case and the case in the Second Circuit: in the Supreme Court, university students were involved, while in the Second Circuit they were in high school. There is some force to the argument that teenagers, who are especially impressionable and in school by force of compulsory attendance laws, should be treated differently from more mature students who voluntarily attend a university. Perhaps that was why, one week after it decided the University of Missouri case, the Supreme Court declined to hear an appeal from Judge Kaufman's decision.

That the Court accepted the principle that minors must be accorded special protection from prayers which were or might seem to be publicly sponsored, was implied in the opinion of another case which the Court declined to hear during the same term.

The Interior Department regularly allowed public property in Washington to be used by groups who sought permission and agreed to defray any special expenses. In 1979, permission was given to the Roman Catholic Church to celebrate a Mass, to be led by the Pope and to be open to the public regardless of religious affiliation, on capitol grounds. The Church would pay for the erection and removal of a platform, an altar, and sound amplification equipment and would provide ushers and portable toilets, while the Interior Department would provide barriers and police for crowd control.

Madalyn Murray, who perhaps had milked her Bible-reading case dry, now sued to have the Papal Mass stopped as a violation of the establishment clause. The Court of Appeals found no violation, noting that the Church was being treated in the same manner as all other groups and that the Mass would be open to everyone, even Mrs. Murray. With respect to Supreme Court decisions disallowing the use of public school property by religious groups, the court held that they were not controlling.

Because of their central and delicate role in American life, and because of the unique susceptibility of their captive audience, children, to coercion, the public schools have a special insulation from religious ceremony.

Under a Louisiana statute the Jefferson Parish School Board decreed a minute of prayer each morning followed by a minute of silent meditation. Elaborate safeguards were provided to assure that no student could possibly be coerced in any way into participating in either exercise. The United States Court of Appeals for the Fifth Circuit held the statute unconstitutional under the establishment clause. *The issue of voluntariness was held to be constitutionally irrelevant.* The Supreme Court affirmed.

CHAPTER XV

The Road Back

THE MOST IMPORTANT vehicle of judicial restraint is the concept of "standing to sue."

The Constitution confers jurisdiction on the federal courts to adjudicate certain categories of "cases" and "controversies." Absent such a case or controversy, federal courts are without any power at all. In acknowledgment of this fundamental restriction, the Supreme Court developed the concept of standing, according to which a plaintiff in a federal court must have more than a general grievance common to all citizens; he must be involved in an actual controversy the outcome of which will have a significant impact on him personally.

The alternative to a "standing" doctrine is to constitute the federal courts ombudsmen with a roving commission, reviewing all acts of the other branches of the federal government, and of all other governments in the United States, and setting aside those it finds unwise. Apart from the sheer impossibility of a few hundred judges undertaking such a monumental task, such a role for appointed officials serving for life is obviously the antithesis of democracy and was never intended by the Founding Fathers.

Perhaps the most surprising feature of the Everson case (discussed in Chapter VII), in which the establishment clause was for the first time extended to the states, was that the issue of standing was not even mentioned. The plaintiffs in that case were taxpayers of New Jersey who objected to governmental subvention of school bus fares to the extent that they benefited the parents of parochial school children. That is precisely the kind of generalized interest, shared with the population at large, which the Supreme Court had previously held insufficient to confer standing to sue. Had the Court adhered to this basic principle of its constitutional mandate, this book could not have been written.

I have mentioned several times that there are fundamental differences between the free exercise clause and the establishment clause. Here is another, for a claim of a violation of free exercise will usually relate to a personal conflict involving the plaintiff himself, and perhaps also an identifiable group of persons similarly situated, while claims under the establishment clause are more likely to involve generalized complaints common to all citizens. *All* the aid-to-education cases could have been avoided by a finding that the plaintiffs, general taxpayers who did not like what their money was being used for, lacked standing to sue. Then the issue could have been returned to the political arena where it could have been decided by democratic processes. But the activist Court of the post-Depression years deemed standing—that is, deemed the case or controversy limitation of the Constitution—a mere technical impediment to the good work it had set out to do. The more modest post-hostage Court has begun to return to first principles.

In 1976, the Secretary of Health, Education and Welfare made a gift of a surplus Veterans Administration hospital with seventy-seven acres of land near Philadelphia to the Valley Forge Christian College, a nonprofit school run by a religious order to train Christian ministers. Americans United for Separation of Church and State, a nonprofit association of some ninety thousand members, sued in federal court to cancel the conveyance as violative of the establishment clause.

The District Court dismissed the complaint on the ground that the plaintiffs, none of whom was involved in any personal dispute over the conveyance (as they might have been, for example, had the value of contiguous property owned by them been adversely affected by the new intended use), lacked standing to sue. The Court of Appeals for the Third Circuit reversed by a two-to-one vote. It noted the standing problem but explained that if citizens could not bring suit in their capacity as citizens, "the Establishment Clause would be rendered virtually unenforceable by the Judiciary."

On January 12, 1982, the Supreme Court reversed, five to four, Justice O'Connor, who had recently joined the Court, providing the swing vote. Justice Rehnquist, who had often been the sole dissenter in religion cases, now wrote the opinion of the Court. He wrote:

> Were the federal courts merely publicly funded forums for the ventilation of public grievances or the refinement of jurisprudential understanding, the concept of 'standing' would be quite unnecessary. But the 'cases and controversies' language of Article III [of the Constitution] forecloses the conversion of the courts of the United States into judicial versions of college debating forums. . . . The federal courts were simply not constituted as ombudsmen of the general welfare.

Six weeks later the Court made the new dispensation manifest in the most dramatic way: it decided a free exercise case *against a fringe group.*

Old Order Amish objected to paying social security taxes on the Scriptural basis of 1 Timothy 5:8 where Paul wrote: "But if anyone does not make provisions for his relations, and especially for members of his own household, he has denied the faith and is worse than an unbeliever." Congress had sought to accommodate the Amish by exempting them from the payment of self-employment social security taxes but had not extended the exemption to Amish employers. An Amish farmer and carpenter who employed other Amish on his farm and in his carpentry shop refused to pay social security taxes for his employees and was assessed for such taxes by the Internal Revenue Service.

The Amish employer sued, claiming that the tax violated his and his employees' free exercise rights. The District Court agreed with him and held the tax unconstitutional. On direct appeal (allowable in certain constitutional cases) the Supreme Court reversed—*unanimously!* Chief Justice Burger wrote for the Court:

> To maintain an organized society that guarantees religious freedom to a great variety of faiths requires that some religious practices yield to the common good. . . . Congress and the courts have been sensitive to the needs flowing from the Free Exercise Clause, but every person cannot be shielded from all the burdens incident to exercising every aspect of the right to practice religious beliefs.

The Court was evidently seeking to enunciate a new, common sense approach to religion clause cases. But if anyone thought the Court had decided to gut the religion clauses, he was soon disabused of that notion.

Grendel's Den was a restaurant in Harvard Square, the commercial hub of Cambridge, Massachusetts. It applied to the Cambridge Licensing Commission for a liquor license. This was denied because of an objection filed by the Holy Cross Armenian Catholic Parish Church, which had a church ten feet away from Grendel's. Under Massachusetts law, a church had an absolute veto power, not subject to any review, over the issuance of a liquor license to any establishment within five hundred feet of the church. Pursuant to this statute, the state Alcoholic Beverages Control Commission affirmed the denial of the license and Grendel's brought suit in federal court claiming, among other things, that the delegation of legislative powers to religious institutions violated the establishment clause of the Constitution.

The District Court agreed with Grendel's. The United States Court of Appeals for the First Circuit disagreed, two to one, and upheld the statute. It found the granting to churches of a veto power over the issuance of liquor licenses to be a reasonable way of providing protection to those churches feeling the need of it without the necessity of a general prohibition. As for the establishment issue, the court noted that the statute had been passed by means of a democratic legislative process and that "it seems to us no gain to replace this democratic process, in which the diverse voices of our society are heard, by the fiat of a handful of judges."

The Chief Judge of the First Circuit dissented. Noting that legislative functions may not even be delegated to elected officials, he agreed with the District Court that the statute's delegation of such power to private individuals was unconstitutional. Moreover, noting that tax exemptions for churches and the deductibility of contributions to them are also available to many nonreligious institutions, and that "I can think of no area where we restrict the receipt of a governmental benefit or privilege solely to a religious group or institution," he agreed that the statute violated the establishment clause.

An extraordinary appellate procedure was now invoked by Grendel's. Federal courts of appeals, regardless of the number of judges in a circuit, always hear cases by three-judge panels. In this case, the panel had been made up of the Chief Judge, who dissented, one other circuit court judge, and a district court judge sitting "by designation." The use of one district judge on a three-man appellate panel is common as a means of reducing appellate backlogs, but in this case the district judge had cast the deciding vote. With that in mind, and in light of the dissent by the Chief Judge, Grendel's now moved for a rehearing *en banc,* that is, before all the judges of the First Circuit. The application was quickly granted and within a few months the Chief Judge was able to convert his dissent into the opinion of the court, while the writer of the original opinion was transformed into the dissenter.

The Supreme Court affirmed by a vote of eight to one. Chief Justice Burger, writing for the Court, noted that a state could ban all liquor sales within the proximity of "churches, schools, hospitals and like institutions," as indeed twenty-seven states did. Such a ban could be outright or subject to hearings where the opinions of the affected institutions could be heard and "would be entitled to substantial weight." But the granting of a standardless, unreviewable veto power to religious institutions, giving the "appearance of a joint exercise of legislative authority by Church and State," violated the establishment clause.

The Grendel decision came down on December 13, 1982. During the first half of 1983 the Court was faced with a few religion cases but they did not seem unusually consequential. For example, the United States Court of Appeals for the Seventh Circuit had held that Jewish basketball players have a constitutional right to wear yarmulkas on public school basketball courts if they can secure them so that they don't fall off during play and create a safety hazard. The Supreme Court let the decision stand. But in the single week of June 29 to July 5, 1983, the Supreme Court rendered two decisions with monumental ramifications for church-state relations in America.

Minnesota passed a statute which allowed parents to deduct from their taxes up to $500 for each child in the sixth grade or under, and up to $700 for each child in the seventh grade or over, based on payments by them to nonprofit private schools or to out-of-district public schools for tuition, textbooks, and transportation. The books must not be used for religious purposes and the schools must adhere to civil rights laws.

It will be remembered that in 1973 the Court had held unconstitutional a New York law which provided tax benefits to low-income parents of children attending private schools. The main difference between that law and the Minnesota law under review was that the New York law limited benefits to low-income families and the schools they attended and provided a tax credit so that its benefits would accrue to all equally, while the Minnesota law made its benefits available to all regardless of income and provided a tax deduction whose value would increase with the income of the beneficiary.

The United States Court of Appeals for the Eighth Circuit upheld the statute. It found a secular purpose: "The manifest purpose of the challenged statute is to provide all taxpayers a benefit which will operate to enhance the quality of education in both public and private schools." That, of course, could be said about any aid program which benefited parochial schools along with public and secular private schools, but many such programs, as we have seen, had been struck down by the Supreme Court.

As for the primary effect of the Minnesota statute, the court referred to a statistical analysis provided by the plaintiffs which showed that the overwhelming tax benefits of the program would be to parents of children in parochial schools. This was because the main component of the program was tuition reimbursement and public school children do not pay tuition (the out-of-district pupils who did pay some tuition were extremely few); and 95 percent of private school children in the state attended parochial schools. Moreover, the Eighth Circuit court noted that the United States Court of Appeals for the First Circuit had recently held a virtually identical Rhode Island statute unconstitutional. Nevertheless, noting that the Supreme Court would have to make the definitive decision, the Eighth Circuit upheld the Minnesota statute on the ground that the benefits conferred by it on parochial schools were much more limited than those conferred upon church institutions by tax exemptions, which the Supreme Court had approved.

Anyone learning that Justice Rehnquist had been assigned the opinion in the case would have been able to anticipate the result —and would have guessed, correctly, that President Reagan's first nominee to the Court, Justice Sandra Day O'Connor, was performing according to expectations. The Court upheld the Minnesota statute by a vote of five to four, Justice O'Connor providing the swing vote (as she had in the "standing" case).

Justice Rehnquist, who had dissented from virtually every decision in which a religious program was invalidated on constitutional grounds, now expressed himself impressed by the grant of tax deductions, not only for children attending private schools, but also for those in out-of-district schools and for certain non-tuition payments for those in regular public schools. Thus he concluded that "this case is vitally different from the scheme struck down in" the New York case.

Justice Marshall, in dissent, was not impressed by the fact that 79 public school pupils, out of a total public school population of 815,000, were eligible for benefits, and contrasted this supposed evenhandedness with the fact that 85,000 parochial school pupils would benefit. He concluded:

> The statute is little more than a subsidy of tuition masquerading as a subsidy of general educational expenses. The other deductible expenses are *de minimus* in comparison to tuition expenses.

Justice Marshall was undoubtedly correct in his assessment of the purpose and primary effect of the Minnesota statute. It remained to be seen whether an outright voucher system of the kind advocated by Milton and Rose Friedman would be allowed, especially where recipients were limited to schools which agreed to adhere to civil rights laws, as beneficiary schools in Minnesota were obliged to do, thereby avoiding the force of the frequently heard argument against vouchers that they would be used to circumvent judicial rulings and legislation designed to create a truly multiracial society. But it could not be gainsaid that the Court had taken an enormous step in the direction of allowing direct governmental support of parochial schools.

But what about prayers?

Robert Palmer was a Presbyterian minister who for sixteen years had been employed by the Nebraska state legislature to say prayers at the beginning of every day's session. He was paid a substantial salary and had his prayers printed, bound, and distributed inside and outside the legislature at public expense. A member of the legislature brought suit in the federal courts to enjoin what he deemed, but had failed to persuade his colleagues was, a blatant establishment of religion, indeed, of *a* religion.

The District Court approved the prayers, noting that it was not unduly concerned with their impact on legislators, who presumably were not unduly impressionable and who, if especially sensitive, could arrange to arrive after Reverend Palmer had completed his invocation. However, the court held that the minister could not receive a governmental salary or have his prayers published at public expense.

The United States Court of Appeals for the Eighth Circuit found the entire business a clearly unconstitutional establishment of religion—indeed, of one religion, the Presbyterian version of Protestant Christianity—and ordered the Nebraska legislature to sack its minister. The Supreme Court reversed by a vote of six to three, Justices Marshall, Brennan and Stevens, representing a dwindling separationist minority on the Court, in dissent.

Chief Justice Burger assigned the opinion to himself. He noted that the opening of legislative bodies in the United States with prayer "is deeply embedded in the history and tradition of this country," and that every session of every federal court, including the Supreme Court, begins with the invocation "God save the United States and this Honorable Court." Accordingly:

In light of the unambiguous and unbroken history of more than 200 years, there can be no doubt that the practice of opening legislative sessions with prayer has become part of the fabric of our society. To invoke Divine guidance on a public body entrusted with making the laws is not, in these circumstances, an "establishment" of religion or a step toward establishment; it is simply a tolerable acknowledgment of beliefs widely held among the people of this country.

Reverend Palmer could keep his job—and, the Chief Justice added, his pay.

Justice Brennan, in dissent, noted that the Chief Justice had failed to apply any of his famous tests of constitutionality under the establishment clause. Had he done so, according to Brennan, he would have had to conclude that there was no secular purpose to the hiring of a chaplain by a legislative body to open its sessions with prayers, that the primary effect of the prayers was obviously religious and not secular, and that "there can be no doubt that the practice of legislative prayer leads to excessive 'entanglement' between the State and religion." "In sum," Brennan wrote, "I have no doubt that, if any group of law students were asked to apply the principles of *Lemon* to the question of legislative prayer, they would nearly unanimously find the practice to be unconstitutional."

Having given the Chief Justice a flunking law school grade on the basis of his own tests, Justice Brennan pointed out that the Court's decision also violated the principles enunciated in the school prayer cases. The Court's historical argument left Brennan unmoved and he thought the reference to the "formulaic recitation" of the invocation with which courts are brought to order to be beside the point. Legislative prayers offered by an ordained minister could readily become sectarian, as the Court's invocation, having remained unchanged for two centuries, obviously was not in danger of doing.

Justice Stevens, also in dissent, was especially disturbed by the possibility of sectarian content in legislative prayers. He noted that Reverend Palmer had on one occasion given the following invocation:

Father in heaven, the suffering and death of your son brought life to the whole world moving our hearts to praise your glory. The power of the cross reveals your concern for the world and the wonder of Christ crucified.

Justice Stevens also noted that the engagement of a single chaplain over a period of sixteen years obviously gave official support to one religion, and he doubted that any state legislature would ever hire a Jehovah's Witness or a Christian Scientist or a member of the Unification Church as its chaplain, demonstrating beyond doubt that the office of legislative chaplain constituted an establishment of a religion in clear violation of the Constitution.

Justice Marshall also dissented, joining Justice Brennan's opinion.

But however cogent and persuasive Brennan's arguments might be, six Justices of the Supreme Court rejected them. It was a shame that the Chief Justice did not openly state that the tripartite establishment clause test he had formulated in Lemon v. Kurtzman, which, as Justice Brennan was certainly correct in noting, required a decision against Reverend Palmer, was no longer to be applied. Nevertheless, it had become clear enough that no legal challenge to any public prayer recited anywhere outside the precincts of a public elementary or high school would have any chance of succeeding for the forseeable future.

There was one last area of church-state relations with which the Court had yet to deal: the public display of religious symbols.

One consequence of the Court's expansion of the establishment clause so as to prohibit nondiscriminatory aid to all religions was the dilemma in which it placed lower courts faced with such issues as displays of religious symbols on public land. If a court found that a religious symbol was indeed involved, it had to order it dismantled. This led to bouts of definitional creativity which brought no honor to the judicial process or to the concerned religions. Thus it was held that a picture of the Virgin Mary on a postage stamp did not "publicize a particular religion," that a fifty-foot Cross "alleged to be representative of the Christian faith" was in fact without religious significance, that a huge lighted stone monument upon which the Ten Commandments were inscribed was "primarily secular, and not religious in character" because "the exact origin of the Ten Commandments is uncertain," and that while it was illegal for a city to permit a private group to maintain a Cross in a public park, it was legal if the city acquired the Cross and called it a "Veterans' War Memorial Cross."

Once a symbol was found to be religious, nothing could save it: a showing that all religions were treated equally was not even *relevant* as a defense under the establishment clause. For example, in Los Angeles it was traditional to display a Latin Cross on City Hall at Christmas and Easter. In 1970 a group of Eastern Orthodox Christians advised the municipal authorities that they celebrated Easter a week later than Western Christians and asked that the Cross be illuminated for their holiday as well. This was done. Then the Heart and Easter Seal campaigns asked that their logos be displayed and their requests were also granted. No other request for the display of a symbol on City Hall was ever made and none was ever denied.

But, in 1978, the California Supreme Court ordered the displays discontinued. "The city hall," declared the court, "is not an immense bulletin board wherein symbols of all faiths could be thumbtacked or otherwise displayed." But why not? Where in the Constitution does it say that a city hall may not be used as a bulletin board? What provision of what Amendment proscribes the public use of thumbtacks? Wasn't the only *constitutional* question whether the municipal bulletin board was made available to all members of the public on a nondiscriminatory basis, as here it clearly was? Yet Chief Justice Bird, in a concurring opinion, wrote that equal treatment in effect compounded the offense, for if many faiths asked that their symbols be displayed, then "passions for and against one or another religion will have become part and parcel of the once neutral experience of travelling within sight of City Hall."

But what in the world was the Chief Justice of California talking about? The record before her showed that there had been an illuminated Cross on City Hall twice a year for a generation. She would have been a little girl when it was last possible to experience a "neutral" City Hall. Nor did she venture to explain why seeing a Cross at Christmas and Easter and a Menorah on Hanukkah and the symbols of other religious faiths on their holidays would stir up divisive passions. It would seem more likely that such an ecumenical display would serve as a salutary reminder that we are a diverse people whose varying faiths enjoy equal governmental respect.

In demonstrable fact, far more divisive passions have been stirred up by lawsuits over displays of religious symbols than by the displays. The prime example involves the crèche, the model of the Nativity scene displayed by many Christians at Christmas time. Can a crèche constitutionally be set down on the lawn of a public school, or the statehouse, or the Ellipse adjacent to the White House?

In the last example, the United States Court of Appeals for the District of Columbia Circuit held that the primary purpose of the Nativity scene in the Christmas display on the Ellipse was to promote tourism in Washington, D.C. There was therefore no constitutional objection to the display. The Lubavitcher Hasidim, an evangelical Orthodox Jewish sect, better understood what was really at stake and proceeded to erect a thirty-foot Menorah in Lafayette Park, across from the White House. But the Court of Appeals obviously felt it necessary to pretend that a model of Mary and Joseph in the manger with the infant Jesus had nothing to do with religion.

But what if local authorities *admitted* that they considered the crèche a religious symbol and that they displayed it on the town hall lawn for the purpose of reminding people that Christmas is not *only* a commercial holiday? Dennis Lynch, the mayor of Pawtucket, Rhode Island, did something close to that a few years ago.

A crèche had been displayed every Christmas in Pawtucket for forty years, along with a Christmas tree, Santa's sleigh, a small village, and a large sign which said "SEASON'S GREETINGS." The display was situated on private land, but it could be seen from the public streets and all the structures were owned and maintained by the city.

No complaints were received by the city until the late fall of 1981 when the American Civil Liberties Union sued to prevent the display of the crèche. (Evidently the Christmas tree and Santa were comparatively inoffensive.) If there had been no divisive passions before, there certainly were now. A Methodist minister denounced the placement of the crèche as demeaning a holy object by putting it next to non-religious objects in an unsuitable atmosphere and a Professor of Philosophy at the University of Rhode Island entered aesthetic objections. A Jewish businessman testified that the display was good for business and he did not mind the crèche. The District Court could not be persuaded that the crèche was truly secular and disallowed it. The United States Court of Appeals for the First Circuit affirmed.

Pawtucket's new mayor, Henry Kinch, virtually dropping the defense of secular purpose, said, "The A.C.L.U. wants to wring every bit of religion out of our daily life." The city appealed. On March 5, 1984, the Supreme Court, considering the issue for the first time, reversed by a five-to-four vote and reinstated the crèche. The Chief Justice, in the majority with Justices White, Powell, Rehnquist, and O'Connor, assigned the opinion to himself.

"In every Establishment Clause case," the Chief Justice wrote, "we must reconcile the inescapable tension between the objective of preventing unnecessary intrusion of either the church or the state upon the other, and the reality that, as the Court has so often noted, total separation of the two is not possible." The Chief Justice then reviewed the history of government involvement with religion, including invocations of Divine guidance, proclamations of days of Thanksgiving, official celebrations of Christmas with paid holidays for federal employees, support of chaplains in the House, Senate, and armed forces, and displays of religious art in publicly owned and maintained galleries. "There is an unbroken history of official acknowledgment by all three branches of government of the role of religion in American life from at least 1789."

Is it then permissible to display religious symbols in public places without pretending they are secular? It is hard to say. For, at the very brink of so deciding, the Chief Justice, perhaps compelled to do so to keep together his bare majority, stepped back and equivocated. "We are satisfied," he wrote, "that the city has a secular purpose for including the crèche, that the city has not impermissibly advanced religion, and that including the crèche does not create excessive entanglement between religion and government."

So it would appear that there must still be a secular purpose to legitimize the public display of a religious symbol. One wonders, though, whether that purpose need be very serious or commensurate with the religious impact of the symbol. After all, the public display of virtually any religious symbol can have the incidental effect of acquainting observers with works of art—a secular purpose, and also with the traditions of some segment of the American people—another secular purpose. It is difficult to think of any religious symbol the public display of which could not meet the Court's new test.

CHAPTER XVI

Impasse

The Minnesota tuition case, the Nebraska legislative chaplain case, and the Rhode Island crèche case were widely hailed as omens presaging a return to the original interpretation of church-state relations. But the high water mark had been reached and soon the Court was to fall back into dissension, confusion, and instransigeance.

Under the Title I program of the Elementary and Secondary Education Act of 1965, federal funds were made available to New York City to pay the salaries of public school teachers and other public employees to provide remedial instruction and counselling to educationally deprived children from low-income families. Most of the children eligible to participate in the New York program attended public schools but 12 percent were parochial school students, both Roman Catholic and Jewish. The public employees travelled to the schools to work with the children but remained entirely separate from the parochial school administration, used materials supplied by the City, and were carefully instructed to keep contacts with the parochial teachers to a minimum. ("Sorry, ma'am, we're not allowed to talk to nuns.")

The District Court found no constitutional infirmity in the program, which had been administered since 1966 without a single reported intrusion of religion into the admittedly secular remedial program. But the Court of Appeals, while agreeing that the program "has done so much good and little, if any, detectable harm," felt obliged by Supreme Court precedents to strike down the use of public funds to pay the salaries of public employees performing services on the premises of parochial schools.

The Supreme Court affirmed by a vote of five to four. Justice O'Connor, dissenting, wrote that for the 20,000 deprived children in New York City thus barred from the program, "the Court's decision is tragic. The Court deprives them of a program that offers a meaningful chance at success in life, and it does so on the untenable grounds that public schoolteachers (most of whom are of different faiths than their students) are likely to start teaching religion merely because they have walked across the threshold of a parochial school."

Chief Justice Burger dissented in even stronger language. He wrote:

> Under the guise of protecting Americans from the evils of an Established Church such as those of the Eighteenth Century and earlier times, today's decision will deny countless schoolchildren desperately needed remedial teaching services funded under Title I. The program at issue covers remedial reading, reading skills, remedial mathematics, English as a second language, and assistance for children needing special help in the learning process. The 'remedial reading' portion of this program, for example, reaches children who suffer from dyslexia, a disease known to be difficult to diagnose and treat . . . . The notion that denying these services to students in religious schools is a neutral act to protect us from an Established Church has no support in logic, experience, or history. Rather than showing the neutrality the Court boasts of, it exhibits nothing less than hostility toward religion and the children who attend church-sponsored schools.

On the same day, by the same vote, the Court also struck down a similar program in Grand Rapids, Michigan.

And still, what about school prayers? It is illegal, we know, in a public school to read verses from the Bible, to recite the Lord's Prayer, or to repeat a nondenominational prayer composed by the school authorities—or not composed by them; and it is illegal to receive religious instruction on the premises of a public school. But what if no one knows what you are doing? What if you pray *silently?*

In 1981, the Alabama legislature passed a statute which provided:

> At the commencement of the first class of each day in all grades in all public schools the teacher in charge of the room in which each class is held may announce that a period of silence not to exceed one minute in duration shall be observed for meditation or voluntary prayer, and during any such period no other activities shall be engaged in.

Twenty-four other states permitted or required public school teachers to have their students observe a moment of silence each morning. But there was something special about the Alabama statute. As Alabama already had a statute providing for a minute of silence at the beginning of each school day, the purpose of the new enactment was clearly to suggest the possibility of using the minute for voluntary prayer. This was admitted at an evidentiary hearing by the state senator who was the prime sponsor of the bill, who testified that his bill was an "effort to return voluntary prayer to our public schools."

A father of three children in the Mobile school system sued. The District Court agreed that under Supreme Court precedents the statute would be unconstitutional, but held that "the United States Supreme Court has erred in its reading of history." The Court of Appeals for the Eleventh Circuit, doubtless wondering what the district judge was smoking, reversed. "Federal district courts and circuit courts," it ruled, "are bound to adhere to the controlling decisions of the Supreme Court. If the Supreme Court errs, no other court may correct it." The Alabama statute was, based on Supreme Court precedents, unconstitutional.

The Supreme Court affirmed by a vote of six to three. It is patently absurd that at this late date the Justices of the Supreme Court cannot agree on what the first clause of the first amendment to the Constitution means, yet this simple case gave rise to six separate opinions: the Court's (written by Justice Stevens), two concurrences (Justices Powell and O'Connor), and three dissents (the Chief Justice and Justices White and Rehnquist)—a total of eighty pages of legal obfuscation.

The Court rested its opinion on Burger's tripartite Lemon test. As Alabama already had a statute providing for a minute of silence at the beginning of each school day, the only purpose of the new enactment, according to the Court, was to permit if not encourage the children to use that minute to say prayers. The statute thus lacked a secular purpose and thereby violated the establishment clause.

The Chief Justice contented himself with a brief dissent in which he wrote: "The notion that the Alabama statute is a step toward creating an established church borders on, if it does not trespass into, the ridiculous." Burger called the majority Justices "naive" (for following *his* test!) and deemed it "bizarre" that "on the very day we heard arguments in this case, the Court's session opened with an invocation for Divine protection." But that was how the Court had always opened its sessions, including the sessions when they heard argument in the Lemon case.

Justice Rehnquist went further. In a thoughtful and scholarly opinion he showed that the Court had lost its way when it elevated Jefferson's casual metaphor of "a wall of separation between church and State" into a principle of constitutional adjudication. The essence of Rehnquist's argument is that the establishment clause was designed to prevent the federal government from establishing a national church or playing favorites among the several religious groups represented in the nation and not to create any hostility between government and religion in general or to place religion and irreligion on an equal level. Rehnquist concluded that a state statute providing a minute of silence for meditation *or prayer* in no way violates that clause. But only two other Justices agreed with him—even Justice O'Connor, President Reagan's appointee, voted to strike down the statute.

At the public high school in Williamsport, Pennsylvania, students attended club activities every Tuesday and Thursday morning for half an hour. There were some twenty-five clubs in operation but those students who preferred could go to the library or to the computer center or could stay in their home rooms. They were required to remain on school property.

A group of students proposed to form a new club which they called "a non-denominational prayer fellowship." 'Participation will be voluntary and open to all students," they assured the school authorities. "The purpose of the organization will be to promote spiritual growth and positive attitudes in the lives of its members." Activities "will include Scripture reading, discussion, prayer and other activities which may be of interest to the group."

No proposal for a student club had ever been denied by the school authorities. Forty-five students showed up for the organizational meeting, which the school permitted, but further meetings were held in abeyance while the school sought advice of counsel. Acting on that advice the president of the School Board wrote to the students:

> Please be assured that neither the School Board nor the Administration regard [sic] the proposed prayer fellowship group as being unworthy. Present law simply does not permit public schools to authorize or support religious activities on school property.

The students took the School Board to court, arguing that their constitutional right of free speech was being violated. They did not even mention free exercise, perhaps hoping to avoid the religious issue altogether. The District Court found for the students, and the School Board, which was not at all averse to a student prayer fellowship, voted eight to one not to appeal. But the dissenting Board member took the case to the Court of Appeals for the Third Circuit, which agreed that the students' right of free speech would be violated if they couldn't meet on school grounds, but held that if the school permitted them to meet for their avowed religious purposes, the school would violate the establishment clause, which in these circumstances must be considered the more important constitutional provision.

In arriving at its decision the Third Circuit relied heavily on Burger's Lemon test. The court conceded that the school's overall club program had a legitimate secular purpose but that to permit *this* club to operate on school property would improperly advance the cause of religion. The court cited the McCollum and Zorach cases and held that if religious instruction on public school property is illegal, as those cases held, then religious exercises on school property must be even more so. The court concluded:

> [T]he Establishment Clause does become implicated when the existence of religion within the school creates the perception among schoolchildren that the State has approved a religious activity and thus has placed its imprimatur on religion. We believe that the danger of communicating such state approval of religion is presented in this case.

The Court of Appeals also found excessive entanglement between the school authorities and religion if the club were permitted to operate, but it did not seem to place much reliance on this finding. As for the nondenominational aspect of the proposed club: "We believe that once an activity is deemed to be 'religious' the degree of partisanship toward a particular denomination does not, and cannot, affect the constitutional analysis."

The court conceded that its decision might seem inconsistent with the Supreme Court's holding that a state university not only could but must permit a student religious group to use its facilities on the same basis as other school groups. But the difference was that the Supreme Court was dealing with college students, who must be deemed mature enough to take care of themselves, while here the court was concerned to protect younger, more vulnerable and impressionable high school students. One judge dissented, insisting that high school students are not all that unduly impressed by what their teacher's say (most high school teachers, who only wish it were otherwise, will confirm that finding), and that as they are in fact exposed to all sorts of influences there is no reason to make a sole exception for religious influences.

The United State Supreme Court announced its decision on March 25, 1986. By a vote of five to four it reversed the Court of Appeals, effectively reinstating the District Court's decision that the students could have their prayer fellowship. One's initial delight in the decision was quickly tempered, however, when one saw that the *dissenting* Justices were Burger, White, Rehnquist, and Powell. What in the world was going on? Then one read the decision of the Court. The separationists had discovered the concept of legal standing! The majority held that as the School Board had voted eight to one not to appeal the decision of the District Court, the lone member who took the case to the Court of Appeals had no standing to sue. Accordingly, the Court of Appeals never had jurisdiction of the case, and its decision was a nullity.

It is an extremely peculiar case which admits of only one conjecture: one of the majority Justices, perhaps Justice O'Connor, was prepared to vote on the merits to allow the religious club but was willing to vote to dismiss for lack of standing. The other majority Justices, who would doubtless have decided the case on the merits if they had the votes to affirm the Court of Appeals, fell back upon the procedural issue as the only way to prevent a decision which would have precedential force. As it is, the case stands for nothing more than that a collegial body cannot be represented in court by a dissenting minority. But it does suggest that there are five Justice on the Supreme Court who believe that public high school students should be allowed to have a prayer fellowship on school property and during school hours.

The Court rendered another decision on March 25, 1986 affecting the religious rights of the American people. Once again it showed that its solicitude for fringe religions does not extend to mainline religions—or perhaps, and I say it with the greatest reluctance, that the Court has a special antipathy for Orthodox Jews.

The reader will recall the blue law cases in which the Court held that Orthodox Jews, whose religion prohibits them from working on Saturday, must comply with a state statute which requires them to cease work also on Sunday, the Christian Sabbath. Those cases were decided in 1961 and held that states have no obligation to exempt observers of other Sabbaths from the operation of Sunday-closing laws. In 1985, the Court went further and held that a Connecticut statute, which provided that *no* person could be required to work on his Sabbath, was unconstitutional. Not only could the states enforce the Christian Sabbath, they could enforce no other—in the name of the establishment clause.

The Court's latest discrimination against Orthodox Jews involved an Air Force officer who wore his yarmulke indoors in violation of Air Force policy. An Orthodox Jew must keep his head covered at all times. Captain Goldman wore his service cap outside, which was proper, but regulations said that no headcovering could be worn indoors except by military police. Goldman was a clinical psychologist, not a policeman, but nobody at the base hospital where he worked made any objection, perhaps because he was an outstanding officer (his evaluation reports consistently found him outstanding in all respects). Then he appeared as a defense witness in a court martial and the prosecutor, who perhaps did not like his testimony, noticed his yarmulke. He was ordered to remove it, he refused, he was threatened with various kinds of disciplinary action, and he sued.

The Supreme Court held five to four that an Orthodox Jew loses his religious rights when he joins the armed forces. The decision for the Court by Justice Rehnquist is cold and unsympathetic, and is based almost entirely on the necessity for deference to the military. He does not weigh in the balance the religious needs of the individual, or note that Captain Goldman was in a noncombat role in a base hospital, or that he wore a yarmulke for four years without objection until he got on the wrong side of a military prosecutor, or that the religious symbol he was required to wear was small and unobtrusive (Goldman's yarmulke was small and the same color as his hair and he offered to substitute any other headcovering the Air Force might prefer).

The Chief Justice simply associated himself with Justice Rehnquist's opinion, but Justices Stevens, White, and Powell, concurring, felt that something more had to be said. Their concern was that while a yarmulke might be inconspicuous, there are symbols of other religions, such as a turban or a saffron robe, which might be incongruous with military duty; and yet the military "has no business drawing distinctions" of that sort. As the military rule barring all visible religious symbols applies to everyone equally, there is no discrimination and no violation of constitutional rights.

Justice Brennan, in dissent with Justices Marshall, Blackmun and O'Connor, was outraged by Justice Rehnquist's rubber-stamp approach to the military and unimpressed with the concurring Justices' concern that accommodating the reasonable needs of an Orthodox Jewish soldier might open the door to unreasonable demands by others. He noted that the military prohibition of all visible religious symbols was not nondiscriminatory but simply favored Christians who are not obliged to wear any. As for the alleged need for uniformity, upon which the Air Force placed great emphasis, Brennan wrote that "a yarmulke worn with a United States military uniform is an eloquent reminder that the shared and proud identity of United States servicemen embraces and unites religious and ethnic pluralism."

What a shame that Justice Brennan's delight in religious and ethnic pluralism stops at the schoolhouse door. But a reading of his opinion in this case, and a comparison of it with Justice, now Chief Justice Rehnquist's, vividly demonstrates that neither side in the ongoing controversy over church-state relations in America has any monopoly of decency, understanding, or tolerance. (Perhaps Justice Rehnquist would have been asked to recuse himself from this case had it then been known, as it was later learned, that he was a party to a deed in which he undertook never to sell his house to "a member of the Hebrew race.")

CONCLUSION

The Golden Rule

———————

THE ESSENCE OF religious freedom in a multisectarian society is, as our Founding Fathers perceived, twofold: (1) freedom from governmental compulsion to worship in any particular way, and (2) freedom to worship in one's own particular way. It was in recognition of this dual aspect of religious freedom that the federal government was explicitly forbidden to establish or disestablish any religion or to interfere with anyone's exercise of his faith.

It is clear that the religion clauses of the First Amendment were never meant to apply to the states—not when the First Amendment was adopted in 1791; not when the Fourteenth Amendment, obliging each state to treat all persons within its jurisdiction equally and with due process of law, was adopted in 1868; and not at any time thereafter, as the repeated defeat of the Blaine Amendment, which would have extended the religion clauses of the First Amendment to the states, demonstrated.

Nearly all of the conflict during the last forty years over the meaning of the religion clauses was the result of the Supreme Court's unilateral and unjustified extension of them to the states.

But religion has not been singled out for discriminatory treatment in this regard. It is merely one of many fields federalized in recent years; the federal government has expanded in all areas far beyond anything the Founding Fathers could have dreamed of—or condoned. Perhaps this was unavoidable, perhaps not. In any event, the desirability or feasibility of reversing so powerful a trend is far beyond the scope of this book. It is certainly too late now to return to the original federal scheme except by means of a constitutional amendment, which is exceedingly unlikely ever to be adopted. It would be foolish and quixotic to discuss the scope of the First Amendment as if it did not apply equally to all governmental authority in the United States—federal, state, and local.

We can therefore define with confidence the first word of the First Amendment: "Congress." It means every governmental authority in the United States, from the federal government in Washington, D.C., to the school board of Champaign, Illinois.

The meaning of the words "shall make no law," as interpreted by the courts, is equally clear and noncontroversial. The phrase means: "shall take no action, whether legislative or executive in nature, having the force of law."

There once was a controversy over the meaning of the word "respecting," but it is now of only historical interest, having to do with the desires of the original states that the federal government should neither establish its own religion nor interfere with their religious establishments. As there are no longer any religious establishments in America, nor any in prospect, the word today has the sole meaning "promoting."

There is one other easy word, "prohibiting." It is clear that a total ban on the exercise of religious faith is not all that is precluded, but any restrictions on worship.

We may therefore rephrase the religion clauses of the First Amendment to read: "Governmental authority, whether federal, state, or local, shall take no action promoting an establishment of religion or inhibiting the free exercise thereof." As a general statement of the meaning of the religion clauses of the First Amendment today, no court would disagree with this phrasing. There is, however, significant disagreement over what is an "establishment of religion" and "the free exercise thereof."

It is possible to narrow the area of controversy. It is clear that, unlike the situation in, say, Britain, the President of the United States is a purely political figure with no religious power whatsoever. Whatever his personal religious convictions and practices, if any, he cannot enforce them in his official capacity. He can be a priest or a rabbi, he can pray on a rug five times a day, but he is not, and constitutionally cannot be, the "defender of the faith." The same goes for the governor of a state or the mayor of a city or a traffic court judge.

The further noncontroversial meaning of the establishment clause is that nobody in the United States can be compelled by any governmental authority to participate in any religious activity. That goes for men, women, children, military cadets or soldiers, government employees, members of Congress, inmates of prisons, and anyone and everyone else, without exception. There may be arguments over, for example, the "subtle pressure" of peers on a school child to join in classroom prayers, but nobody has ever suggested that any child could constitutionally be compelled by the school administration to say prayers against his will.

At the other end of the religious freedom spectrum, no person in the United States can be prevented by governmental authority from going to church, synagogue or mosque or otherwise engaging in worship when and how he wishes. Certain practices have been outlawed as contrary to public morals, notably polygamy, and it is unlikely that the sacrifice of virgins would be permitted. But within the broad confines of the criminal laws applicable to all citizens, Americans can follow any form of religion, from those in the mainline Judaeo-Christian tradition to the most exotic cults of undeterminable provenance.

All of the above is noncontroversial. That alone is a near miracle, a state of affairs nearly unprecedented in human history, a cause for great pride in Americans. But some questions remain open: mainly, (1) what is an establishment of religion? which government may not promote, and (2) what is the free exercise thereof? which government may not inhibit.

One additional question has caused much trouble, and it may be desirable to deal with it before tackling the big questions. It is: What is "religion'? and: Is "religion" in the establishment clause the same concept as "religion" in the free exercise clause?

Grammatically, we are dealing with a single concept. This formal equation was seized upon by the four dissenting judges in the case where a town in New Jersey was permitted to reimburse parents of parochial school children for their bus fares. Since parents are constitutionally *entitled* to send their children to parochial school, the dissenters argued, government must be constitutionally *prohibited* to help them do so.

There is little question but that to the Founding Fathers "religion" did essentially have one meaning: the beliefs and practices associated with the worship of God, whether the Christian God, the Jewish God, nature's God, or Divine Providence. With that broad definition, and with the concomitant understanding, which the Founding Fathers also shared, that the only thing prohibited by the establishment clause of the First Amendment was *compulsion* of worship or the *preferential* treatment of one religion over competing religions, there would be little trouble today over interpretation and application of the establishment clause, and little "tension" between it and the free exercise clause.

But the Supreme Court greatly expanded both the definition of "religion" and the scope of the prohibitions of the establishment clause, with the result that an impasse, the classical irresistible force meeting immovable object, was created. As phrased by the Court, "tension inevitably exists between the Free Exercise and the Establishment clauses." But there was nothing inevitable about it.

There are good reasons for expanding the definition of "religion" to include virtually anything anybody deems sacred. The alternative puts the courts in the business of defining and assessing professed religious beliefs, a business for which they are neither equipped nor suited. If Henry David Thoreau occupies a place in a person's life comparable to that occupied by God in the life of a believer (the Supreme Court's phraseology in the conscientious objector cases), there seems no good reason why *Walden* should not enjoy all the protections accorded sacred scripture. But this special status extended to a writing under the free exercise clause will be a cruel joke if *as a consequence* it ends up on the establishment clause index.

Actually, if establishment continued to be defined as compulsion or preferential treatment, religion could be defined as broadly as might be desired. The "tension" only appears when the definition of religion is broadened for free exercise purposes *and* it is held that any governmental aid of religion, no matter how evenhanded, is prohibited by the establishment clause. *Then* it is inevitable that there will be tension between what the free exercise clause *requires* and what the establishment clause *forbids.*

The courts have become, if rather late in the day, fully aware of this dilemma. When, in 1973, the Supreme Court struck down a New York plan to reimburse low-income families for parochial school tuition, it admitted that "it may often not be possible to promote the [free exercise clause] without offending the [establishment clause]." Similarly, when in 1980 the United States Court of Appeals for the Second Circuit held that the establishment clause required a public high school to deny the request of students to be allowed to hold prayer meetings on school grounds before the beginning of the school day, it conceded that the denial would violate their free exercise rights.

The preference of the courts for the establishment clause over the free exercise clause has given rise to much comment. It has been observed that free exercise is the goal of *both* of the religion clauses, the prohibition of establishment merely constituting a necessary means by which to realize it. According to this interpretation, whenever tension appears between the clauses, free exercise should prevail. Professor Laurence Tribe of Harvard Law School, one of the foremost constitutional scholars of today, has put it this way:

> Whenever a free exercise claim conflicts with an absolute non-establishment theory, the support of the former would be more faithful to the consensus present at the time of the Constitutional Convention and of the First Congress.

In other words, the trouble is not an "inevitable" conflict between the clauses, obliging us to choose between them, but the "absolute non-establishment theory" to which Professor Tribe refers. The rigid prohibition of every form of governmental aid of religious endeavor and expression, never intended by the Founding Fathers, of course results in tension with any sensible definition of free exercise. Indeed, the very tension referred to by the courts should suggest to them that something may be amiss in their treatment of the religion clauses.

That brings us to the central questions: (1) What is an establishment of religion? and (2) What is the free exercise thereof? It seems to me, after reading what Jefferson and Madison wrote on the subject, studying the cases, state and federal, and considering the observations of legal scholars of varying predilections, that there really should be no serious disagreement over the meaning of either of the religion clauses of the First Amendment.

The free exercise clause is perhaps the simpler one to understand, so I will consider it first. In essence it means that, consistent with public morals and an orderly society, every person should be allowed, and wherever possible helped, to worship whatever it is he deems sacred in whatever manner he deems appropriate. The qualifying phrase, "consistent with public morals and an orderly society," should be and usually has been interpreted to require a showing of significant public harm to justify inhibiting a religious practice. Thus an Indian tribe was permitted to use an hallucinatory drug in its rituals despite its general proscription as a "controlled substance," Old Order Amish were permitted to remove their children from school at fourteen despite a state statute requiring school attendance until sixteen, and Jehovah's Witness children were permitted to abstain from pledging allegiance to the flag, which their religion held was a graven image, but no exemptions from the general laws were granted to polygamists or to Amish employers who did not wish to pay social security taxes for their employees (Amish had been granted a *statutory* exemption from paying social security taxes for themselves).

The cases refusing an exemption from Sunday-closing laws to persons observing a strict Saturday Sabbath were, I submit, wrongly decided and placed a harsh and improper burden on the religious practices of Jews, Moslems, Seventh-Day Adventists and the adherents of other religions observing a Sabbath on a day other than the day observed by Christians. The argument made in those cases by the states concerned and accepted by the Supreme Court, that administration of exemptions for non-Sunday Sabbatarians would be so cumbersome as to be unworkable, was patently specious, as shown by the existence of just such exemptions in many other states; and the Court's subsequent ruling that a state's attempt to recognize *everybody's* Sabbath was in violation of the establishment clause, was deeply disquieting, as was its decision that an Orthodox Jewish officer can be compelled to violate the tenets of his religion if ordered to remove his yarmulke. But the decisions in these cases did not result from theoretical misconceptions with wider ramifications. They resulted from insensitivity on the part of some Justices to the religious needs of individuals with whom they lacked sympathy.

The free exercise clause, then, interpreted broadly and applied with common sense and goodwill, should not give rise to serious problems. Establishment clause cases are inherently more difficult; yet they too could be decided with relative ease with the application of a bit more common sense and goodwill than has been in evidence in judicial decisions striking down nondiscriminatory public assistance programs.

As discussed in Chapter XV, the Supreme Court, in 1983, upheld a state statute providing reimbursement of parochial school tuition. But the Court was obliged to accomplish this result by means of a disingenuous acceptance of a far-fetched rationale of universality; and even that rationale failed when the Court struck down attempts to provide deprived children in New York City and Grand Rapids, Michigan, parochial and public school students alike, with remedial services.

But why shouldn't a nondiscriminatory program of public support of all schools within a jurisdiction, public, secular private, and church-sponsored, be allowed? In other words, let us consider the extreme case where a state offers its citizens educational vouchers redeemable at any school meeting state accreditation requirements. Such a system has been advocated, notably by Milton and Rose Friedman, and has been opposed with great vehemence by the educational establishment. Should the political processes by which such a program could be adopted or rejected be short-circuited by a judicial holding that it would be unconstitutional under the establishment clause because aid would be given to parochial schools along with public and secular private schools?

The issue of *compulsion* can be quickly disposed of. No one under a voucher program would be obliged to attend a parochial school, much less any particular parochial school. Indeed, the issue of school prayers, usually considered under the rubric of compulsion, would be significantly defused if children could attend any school they desired. If prayers were important, then, a child could be sent to a school which said them; and the counterparts of Terry McCollum and William Murray could go, with children of similarly-minded parents, to a school which didn't.

The issue of *preferential treatment* of one religion over others would seem as easily disposed of. In a scheme of vouchers redeemable at any accredited school, no issue of preference could arise. The argument that such a scheme would primarily benefit the Catholic Church, because most parochial schools are Catholic, completely misconstrues the purpose of the establishment clause. It might as well be argued that maintaining the roads favors Catholics because they use them to go to church more often than Protestants, Jews, or Madalyn Murray, or that lower postal rates for books supports southern Baptists who mail so many Bibles. As long as equal benefits are available to all religions, a scheme is not rendered unconstitutionally preferential because one or more religious groups choose not to take equal advantage of it.

There would thus appear to be *no* establishment clause reason why an educational voucher system should not be sponsored by a state. (There might be an equal protection clause reason if such a system tended to result in racially segregated schools, but that could be dealt with, as it was in the tuition reimbursement scheme allowed by the Court, by requiring that beneficiary schools agree to adhere to civil rights legislation.) Yet I fear that the Court, even as constituted today, would have difficulty in allowing such a program.

Why? Because of Justice Black's formulation of the establishment clause forty years ago:

> The "establishment of religion" clause of the First Amendment means at least this: Neither a state nor the Federal Government can set up a church. Neither can pass laws which aid one religion, *aid all religions,* or prefer one religion over another.

The answer to Justice Black is that he was wrong, and that forty years of adherence by the Supreme Court to a wrong theory is enough. As stated by a leading American legal scholar:

The historical record shows beyond peradventure that the core idea of "an establishment of religion" comprises the idea of *preference;* and that any act of public authority favorable to religion in general cannot, without manifest falsification of history, be brought under the ban of that phrase."

There remains but one church-state issue to consider: religious activities in public schools—prayers, Bible recitations, hymn singing, Christmas and Hanukkah pageants, grace before milk and cookies. No discussion of church-state relations in America can be complete without a candid discussion of this difficult issue, and it should be noted at the outset that there are men and women of goodwill on both sides, and that reference to the Founding Fathers is of limited assistance as the first public high school was founded in 1821 (in Boston) and public schools were not widespread in the United States until after the Civil War.

The arguments in favor of school religious exercises boil down to a belief that spiritual values must be inculcated in our children and that the home and the church are unequal to the job. The principal argument against them is that religion in our pluralistic society is essentially divisive and must be kept out of the public schools, which have been a major vehicle for creating a cohesive society.

I think the proponents of school prayers expect too much from them, and the opponents fear them too much. Both sides exaggerate the significance of what inevitably must be a rather formal exercise necessarily drained of deep meaning by the requirement of sectarian neutrality. Nevertheless, a major literature could be created from the eloquence and passion with which the issue has been discussed. It evidently means a lot to many people, and in a democracy, that matters.

But the issue must be discussed against the background of the First Amendment, not, as is too often the case, in a vacuum. The idea that secular or "humanistic" ideals are entitled to the same constitutional consideration as religious principles, or that agnosticism and even atheism must be given equal constitutional billing with traditional religion, is simply false. All forms of expression enjoy constitutional protection under the free speech and press clauses of the First Amendment, but religion enjoys something more: the free exercise thereof. The argument that to give nondiscriminatory aid to all religions is to discriminate against irreligion has as its effect, if not its purpose, the emptying of the free exercise clause of any meaning whatsoever.

But the basic weakness of the strict separationist position on school prayers is that it is not honest. It is fascinating how the same people who on certain occasions profess great sympathy for minorities and poor people turn into Marie Antoinette when confronted with school prayers: let them go to private school, or let their parents teach them religion. How can a person who in the context of aid to dependent children cites statistics of broken homes, rodent-infested apartments crowded beyond imagination, and children roaming the streets untended, in the context of school prayers conjure up warm families sitting around the fireside listening to the paterfamilias (50 percent of minority children in the United States live in fatherless homes) recite verses from the Bible with appropriate commentary?

But middle-class children from two-parent families may not receive much more religious training at home than ghetto children. The image of the patriarchical family reading the Bible (or anything else) around the hearth is nearly as fanciful in the suburbs as in the central city. Only judges of venerable age and advanced myopia can suppose that there is time and occasion in the modern middle-class home for morning prayers. In the real world the weekday morning is a paradigm of chaos—of father racing about shaving, searching for the one tie he really likes with this suit, gulping a doughnut and coffee, grabbing his briefcase, and rushing off to catch the 7:07; of mother trying to feed everyone (maybe even herself), dress herself and the five-year-old, search for the ten-year-old's math paper, assure the thirteen-year-old that she did not hide his sneakers, drive the children to school(s) and/or bus stop(s), and perhaps also get to her job on time (half of American mothers hold jobs outside the home). In this frenetic, frantic atmosphere, the possibility of stopping everything for three minutes to calm the spirit and give thanks to something beyond ourselves that, while millions are cold and hungry and despairing, our worst problems are finding ties, math papers and sneakers, is remote.

After-school opportunities for familial contemplation of eternity are even fewer. Extracurricular activities consume most of the children's time before dinner, shopping and cooking and perhaps her job consume all of mother's, and father is lucky if he makes it home for dinner. And then there is the ubiquitous television set by means of which the children will be taught that happiness may be found, may *only* be found, through the acquisition of nonessentials—a toy, a vacation, a car capable of going 120 mph in a country with a 55 mph speed limit. They see grown men and women exploding with joy because they guessed the price of an appliance they do not need and will now be given; they see fairytale children playing blissfully in an enchanted land and are told that their palpable joy derives from chewing a certain brand of gum; they see portrayals of camaraderie, of intimacy and sharing among handsome men and lovely women untouched by sickness or human frailty in a pastoral idyll based solely on the consumption of a certain brand of beer.

With what in their lives can our middle-class children, much less our ghetto children, compare the moments of face-splitting joy, the perpetual epiphanies, they see on TV? When have they known the pure bliss of the prize winners, the gum chewers, or the beer drinkers? They may not need a refrigerator or a microwave oven, they have chewed truckloads of gum with little effect on anything but their teeth, and if they're old enough to drink beer they know that Lowenbrau was turned into just another American beer when Miller bought the ancient German name. But they can imagine one day wanting a refrigerator or anyway a Corvette, they can readily imagine ingesting something which will provide great joy (doubtless they can find purveyors of things more powerful than gum in the schoolyard—the feds are much better at stopping prayers than drug peddlers), and they can surely hope to find a better beer when they are up to that. What they know now, and know in the vitals of their being, know as firmly as a Jew or a Christian or a Moslem knows there is a God, is that happiness, health and friendship come from *things.*

That, your Honor, is what children learn at home. Perhaps religious faith is a sham, "a chronic disease of the imagination contracted in childhood," the opium of the people. Perhaps Charlie's angels have more to offer than those Billy Graham writes about. But if you think so, why not say so? To pay lip service to the "spiritual needs of our young people" and then tell them that they must seek their fulfillment at home and only at home, is ignorant or dishonest or both.

Sex must be taught in the schools because parents are unequal to the task, but religious instruction is held to be within their competence. Surely the evidence compels the opposite conclusion.

The argument that, like Sergeant Friday in the old *Dragnet* series, schools are only concerned with *facts,* is equally untenable. The selection and presentation of the limitless supply of available observations, theories, and opinions determine the direction and meaning of the educational process. George Washington was born in 1732. So was Haydn. So, no doubt, were many other people, including saints and sadists and blasphemers and traitors. All *facts,* but which will you disinter and teach? Obviously it depends upon your animating principles. The Founding Fathers were animated by a belief in Divine Providence, a faith broad enough to take in theism and even, perhaps, pantheism, along with traditional religions. Some of us are still animated by similar beliefs, others are busy looking out for "Number 1," and still others are totally immersed in the beliefs and rituals of ancient religions. The one thing we should all be able to agree upon is that the courts should not take sides in the ongoing debate.

But what about prayers? The Court has now held that prayers may be said at the beginning of legislative and judicial sessions and one may suppose that the executive enjoys equal rights; and every President from Washington to Reagan has invoked divine assistance at his inauguration. It has also held that students at a state university have a *right* to hold prayer meetings on school premises, and at least four Justices would extend that right to public high school students. But, largely as a result of Chief Justice Burger's tripartite establishment clause test, prayers are still banned from all public elementary and high schools in the country.

It should be understood that the ban is virtually total. For example, in 1982 the Tennessee legislature was considering a bill to allow (not require) public schools to set aside time for—well, for whatever the courts would allow. It had before it a statute drawn up by the Georgia legislature according to which a school could set aside up to three ten-minute periods a day—before school, after school, or during the lunch break—where students who so desired could use an empty classroom for prayers or silent meditation. The attorney general of Tennessee advised the legislature that the statute was unconstitutional. After several tries the legislature finally agreed on one minute of silence at the beginning of the school day and included in the statute a warning that teachers were not to suggest what the students should be thinking about during that minute. Even this statute was submitted to the attorney general for an opinion. He reviewed the cases, noted that "It is well-settled that the Establishment Clause forbids the state from requiring or even condoning perceptible religious exercises in public schools," and said that as long as the teachers did not encourage the students to say prayers during the minute of silence, the statute was constitutional. The Supreme Court's subsequent decision in the Alabama silent-prayer case shows that the Tennessee attorney general's warnings were well taken.

But isn't it ridiculous? Any attempt to restrict the availability of obscene, racist novels in public school libraries is immediately attacked as Nazism in the making; public school students are held to have a constitutional right to select their dress and hairstyles and to demonstrate in class against governmental policies of which they disapprove; but *God* has become so terrible a word that all the legal talent in the country must be mustered to exclude it absolutely from the public schools.

It is true that America's religions did not always live together in peace and harmony. The Puritans were not known for their tolerance of dissenters, anti-Catholic agitation once disfigured a large part of our public life, and no one named Goldberg is unaware of the history of anti-Semitism in America. But it is equally true that the tables have turned 180 degrees, and shields have been transformed into swords. In the words of a Jesuit scholar:

> There has been a full and truly vicious circle, from religious persecution, intolerance and church establishment to benign tolerance; to disestablishment; to equality of all faiths before the law; to equality of belief and nonbelief before the law; and now to the secularists' and

the religious dissenters' intolerance of religious belief in public law. The wry irony is that this is being done in the name of and for the sake of religious liberty.

The Supreme Court's abuse of the establishment clause over the past forty years has generated a national conflict of epic proportions—precisely what the Founding Fathers designed the First Amendment to avoid. "The Court's misinterpretation of the establishment clause," writes Richard E. Morgan, professor of constitutional law at Bowdoin College and chairman of its department of government, "is now an open scandal." But as the Court of Appeals for the Eleventh Circuit held in the Alabama silent prayer case, "If the Supreme Court errs, no other court may correct it." There is only one way of correcting the Supreme Court: by amending the Constitution, even if only to add the words "And we mean it."

Polls consistently show that 80 percent or more of the American people want religious exercises in their public schools. Accordingly, proposed constitutional amendments have been introduced in Congress, such as H.J. Res. 279:

> Nothing in this Constitution shall be construed to prohibit individual or group prayer in public schools or other public institutions. No person shall be required by the United States or by any State to participate in prayer. Neither the United States nor any State shall compose the words of any prayer to be said in public schools.

Neither this proposed amendment nor any other has yet been voted on by either House but there is mounting pressure for something to be done. It would be most unfortunate if an amendment should prove necessary, for it will only usher in another generation of conflict over interpretation and application.

For example, H.J. Res. 279 does not require that prayers in public schools must be nondenominational or that if sectarian that various religious groups are entitled to recognition. There is no limitation as to time, and whereas a school is not permitted to compose the words of a prayer, there is no express prohibition on it engaging the services of a priest or a rabbi to do so, and to conduct the exercises. The proposed amendment would seem to permit a Catholic priest to celebrate the Mass at a public school or a rabbi to conduct an entire Passover seder there. Can anyone doubt that such an amendment should be subtitled *Constitutional Lawyers' Relief Act?*

But we are a democracy and the overwhelming majority of Americans want religious exercises in their public schools. If the Constitution must be amended for their desires to be respected, then I would suggest a much simpler formulation:

> Nothing in this Constitution shall be construed to prohibit public schools from conducting or permitting a brief nondenominational prayer at the start of each school day.

Intolerance is ugly, no matter who practices it. When a minority practices it, it is also foolhardy, for intolerance breeds more intolerance, and minorities naturally suffer the most from an atmosphere of intolerance. With tolerance for the beliefs and practices of others, however foolish they may seem, and enlisting the aid of the courts not to prevent others from doing what they want but only to enforce one's own right to equal time, the issue of prayers in public school could be resolved tomorrow.

Nearly a century and a half ago, New York's Superintendent of Schools, faced with this very issue, put the solution in terms I think cannot be improved upon:

> Both parties have rights; the one to bring up their children in the practice of publicly thanking their Creator for His protection, and invoking His blessing; the other of declining in behalf of their children, the religious services of any person in whose creed they may not concur, or for other reasons satisfactory to themselves. These rights are reciprocal, and should be protected equally; and neither should interfere with the other. Those who desire that their children should engage in public prayer have no right to compel other children to unite in the exercise, against the wishes of their parents. Nor have those who object to this time place or manner of praying, or to the person who conducts the exercises, a right to deprive the other class of the opportunity of habituating their children to what they conceive an imperious duty. Neither the common school system, nor

any other social system, can be maintained, unless the conscientious views of all are equally respected. The simple rule, so to exercise your own rights as not to infringe on those of others, will preserve equal justice among all, promote harmony, and insure success to our schools.

Guide to Legal Research

THE FEDERAL COURT system is three-tiered. At the bottom are 94 District Courts, at least one for each state, the District of Columbia, Puerto Rico, and the territories under United States administration. All federal cases begin at this level. Appeals are taken, as a matter of right, to the Court of Appeals in each circuit, of which there are eleven. (Most circuits cover contiguous states but the judges of the frigid First Circuit, which includes Maine, Massachusetts, New Hampshire and Rhode Island, also get to sit in San Juan.) At the top of the pyramid, in lonely splendor in its own marble building just east of the Capitol, sits the Supreme Court.

(There are additional specialized federal courts which will not be dealt with here as they were not involved in any of the cases cited in this book. These include the Court of Claims, the Customs Court, the Court of Customs and Patent Appeals, the Court of Military Appeals, and the Tax Court.)

All federal judges are nominated by the President, confirmed by the Senate, and serve until they die, retire or are impeached by a majority of the House of Representatives and convicted by two-thirds of the Senate. For all practical purposes, federal judges sit for life, including, in many instances, periods of senility.

District Court judges are the trial judges of the federal system. One district judge, with or without a jury, presides over all federal trials (except where a constitutional issue is raised, when a special three-judge District Court may be convened). The decisions of all federal district courts (including three-judge constitutional courts) are reported in the Federal Supplement, abbreviated "F. Supp." An example of a District Court citation is: United States v. Ballard, 35 F. Supp. 105 (S.D.Cal. 1940). This tells you that you will find the case named United States v. Ballard, decided by the United States District Court for the Southern District of California in 1940, in volume 35 of the Federal Supplement at page 105. Some District Court cases (starting with 1938) are reported in Federal Rules Decisions (F.R.D.), and all District Court cases before 1932 were reported together with Courts of Appeals cases in the Federal Reporter.

All federal Courts of Appeals are three-judge courts. There may be many more federal appellate judges in a busy circuit like the Second (which covers Connecticut, New York, and Vermont) or the Ninth (which covers Alaska, Arizona, California, Hawaii, Idaho, Montana, Nevada, Oregon, Washington, and Guam) but only three will sit on a panel. An application can be made by a party dissatisfied with the decision of a regular three-judge panel for a rehearing *en banc*—that is, by all the judges of the circuit—but it is rarely granted. The decisions of all federal Courts of Appeals are reported in the Federal Reporter. An example of a citation to a Court of Appeals decision is United States v. Ballard, 138 F.2d 540 (9th Cir. 1943). This tells you that you will find the decision of the United States Court of Appeals for the Ninth Circuit in the case of United States v. Ballard, rendered in 1943, in volume 138 of the Federal Reporter, Second Series, at page 540.

The United States Supreme Court hears all cases *en banc*—that is, the entire nine-judge court sits in every case that comes before the Court (except where a Justice "recuses" himself—that is, declines to sit because of some disqualifying relationship with the subject matter of the case or with one of the parties or counsel). A party dissatisfied with a decision of a United States Court of Appeals can petition the Supreme Court to hear an appeal. The Supreme Court grants a small percentage of such petitions. Its denial of a petition carries some weight, though not as much as an affirmance, though the immediate effect is the same. In certain special categories of cases, such as decisions of three-judge constitutional District Courts, appeal may be had directly to the Supreme Court. All decisions of the Supreme Court are officially reported in the volumes of the United States Reports, sold (at bargain prices) by the Government Printing Office. An example of a citation to the United States Reports is: United States v. Ballard, 322 U.S. 78 (1944). There are also two unofficial Supreme Court reporters, Supreme Court Reporter (S.Ct) and Lawyers' Edition (L.Ed.). Smaller libraries tend to keep one of the unofficial reporters because they take up less room than the official reporter, and because they provide indexing systems not available in the official reporter. Citation to the official reporter is the preferred form and is the form required in briefs submitted to federal courts.

In addition to the bound volumes of federal reporters there is a looseleaf service called United States Law Week, abbreviated U.S.L.W., which keeps lawyers up-to-the-minute on all cases pending and decided in the federal courts. It is only cited when no other report has yet been published.

Forms of citation to decisions of state courts differ from state to state. Nevertheless, in all instances the same format is used: 000 XXX 111 (YYY, 2222), where 000 = volume number, XXX = name of reporter (including series, where applicable), 111 = page number, YYY = name of court (but references to the highest court in the state are usually omitted), and 2222 = the year in which the decision was rendered.

For a complete guide to citations to all federal and state cases, statutes, administrative rulings, legislative materials, and the like, see the current edition of *A Uniform System of Citation* published jointly every few years by the Columbia Law Review, The Harvard Law Review, the University of Pennsylvania Law Review, and the Yale Law Journal.

There are various indexes to federal and state cases to assist researchers in finding cases on a certain subject and to facilitate tracing the history of a specific case. The librarian in any law library is able to demonstrate how to use the indexes available in that library. Today there are also two computer services, Lexis and Westlaw, available in many law libraries. They take some getting used to, as scanning takes the place of indexing, and they can be quite expensive if used extensively; but it is possible to do things with them that cannot be done with any other resource. Again, any library that has a computer will have someone in attendance who knows how to use it, and computer searches may usually be purchased for a fee.

Finally, if you want to have a limitless supply of fascinating reading for train, plane, or bedtime, subscribe to the preliminary prints of the United States Reports, obtainable from the Superintendent of Documents, U.S. Government Printing Office, Washington, D.C. 20402. At the time of this writing the cost is $76 per term of Court.

Sources

FRONTISPIECE

Neely, *How Courts Govern America* (1981), p. 18.

Baritz, *Backfire* (1985), p. 339.

CHAPTER I

Religious tests for federal office are prohibited by Article VI, Section 3 of the Constitution.

The quotation from Chief Justice Marshall is taken from his opinion in Barron v. Baltimore, 32 U.S. (7 Pet.) 243, 249 (1833).

Article I, Section 2, para. 3 of the Constitution, which provides for the apportionment of members of the House of Representatives according to population, excludes "Indians not taxed" from the census and adds to all "free Persons, including those bound to Service for a Term of Years," "three fifths of all other Persons." It is interesting that the Founding Fathers chose not to specify Negro slaves by name; but that is what they meant.

For material on the Blaine Amendment, see Meyer, "The Blaine Amendment and the Bill of Rights," 64 Harvard Law Review 939 (1951) and Rice, *The Supreme Court and Public Prayer* (1964). The Congressional debates over the Blaine Amendment may be found in 4 Cong. Rec. 5580 et seq. (1876).

CHAPTER II

Moore v. Monroe, 64 Iowa 367, 20 N.W. 475 (1884).

Weiss v. District Board, 76 Wis. 177, 44 N.W. 967 (1890).

Pfeiffer v. Board of Education, 118 Mich. 560, 77 N.W. 250 (1898).

Freeman v. Scheve, 65 Neb. 853, 91 N.W. 846 (1902).

Billard v. Board of Education, 69 Kan. 53, 76 Pac. 422 (1904).

Hackett v. Brooksville Graded School District, 120 Ky. 608, 87 S.W. 792 (1904).

Twining v. New Jersey, 211 U.S. 78, 98–99 (1908). Justice Frankfurter's characterization of the opinion is from his concurring opinion in Adamson v. California, 332 U.S. 46, 59 (1947).

Church v. Bullock, 104 Tex. 1, 109 S.W. 115 (1908).

Ring v. Board of Education, 245 Ill. 334, 92 N.E. 251, 252 (1910).

Herold v. Parish Board of School Directors, 136 La. 1034, 68 So. 116 (1915).

Wilkerson v. City of Rome, 152 Ga. 763, 110 S.E. 895 (1922).

Prudential Insurance Co. v. Cheek, 259 U.S. 530, 543 (1922).

Pierce v. Society of the Sisters of the Holy Names of Jesus and Mary, 268 U.S. 510, 534–35 (1925).

Wisconsin v. Yoder, 406 U.S. 205, 233 (1972).

CHAPTER III

Gitlow v. New York, 268 U.S. 652, 666 (1925).

Whitney v. California, 274 U.S. 357 (1927). The Brandeis quotation is at 373.

Marbury v. Madison, 5 U.S. (1 Cranch.) 137 (1803).

The red flag case was Stromberg v. California, 283 U.S. 359 (1931). The quotation is at 369.

De Jonge v. Oregon, 299 U.S. 353, 364–65 (1937).

Palko v. Connecticut, 302 U.S. 319, 323 (1937).

CHAPTER IV

Kaplan v. Independent School District, 171 Minn. 142, 214 N.W. 18 (1927).

Finger v. Weedman, 226 N.W. 348 (S.D. 1929).

Clithero v. Showalter, 159 Wash. 519, 293 Pac. 1000, 1002 (1930).

Gerhardt v. Heid, 66 N.D. 444, 267 N.W. 127 (1936).

The double jeopardy case was Palko v. Connecticut, 302 U.S. 319 (1937), discussed in Chapter III.

The best account of the Witnesses' many legal battles is Manwaring, *Render Unto Caesar: The Flag Salute Controversy* (1962), upon which much of the background material in this chapter is based.

The intemperate language used by the Witnesses in reference to the Catholic Church is quoted in the concurring/dissenting opinion of Justice Jackson in Douglas v. City of Jeannette, 319 U.S. 157, 171 (1943).

Lovell v. City of Griffin, 303 U.S. 444 (1938).

The Supreme Court case involving ordinances in Los Angeles, Milwaukee and Worcester was Schneider v. State, 308 U.S. 147 (1939).

Cantwell v. Connecticut, 310 U.S. 296 (1940). The Court's description of the neighborhood which the Cantwells canvassed is at 301, the Court's holding is at 303. The Time description is in the issue of April 8, 1940 at p.35, where the quotations from the phonograph record and the oral argument in the Supreme Court are set forth.

CHAPTER V

For the background of the flag salute cases see Manwaring, *Render Unto Caesar: The Flag Salute Controversy* (1962).

The Witnesses' alternative pledge is quoted in West Virginia State Board of Education v. Barnette, 319 U.S. 624, 628 n.4 (1943).

The decision of the District Court in the Gobitis case is reported at 21 F. Supp. 581 (E.D.Pa. 1937), of the Court of Appeals at 108 F.2d 683 (3d Cir. 1939), of the Supreme Court at 310 U.S. 586 (1940). The quotation from Justice Frankfurter's opinion is at 596, from Justice Stone's dissenting opinion at 603–4. The quotations from the notes to Justice Frankfurter of Justices Douglas, Murphy and Roberts are taken from Hirsch, *The Enigma of Felix Frankfurter* (1981), p. 150.

The "chief historian of the Witnesses' constitutional struggles" is Manwaring, cited above.

Cox v. New Hampshire, 312 U.S. 569, 574 (1941).

The case involving ordinances in Alabama, Arkansas and Arizona was Jones v. City of Opelika, 316 U.S. 584 (1942). The quotation from Justice Reed's opinion is at 599, from the dissenters' at 624.

Frankfurter's "recent biographer" is Hirsch, cited above, p. 141. Frankfurter's comment on his lack of ties to formal religion is at p. 169.

The peddlers' license case which was reversed shortly after Justice Rutledge joined the Court was Jones v. City of Opelika, 319 U.S. 103 (1943). See also the companion cases decided the same day, Murdock v. Commonwealth of Pennsylvania, 319 U.S. 105 and Martin v. City of Struthers, 319 U.S. 141.

The decision of the District Court in the Barnette case is reported at 47 F. Supp. 251 (S.D.W.Va. 1942), of the Supreme Court at 319 U.S. 624 (1943). The quotation from Justice Black's opinion is at 644, from Justice Murphy's at 646, from Justice Jackson's at 641. Justice Frankfurter's dissent is at 646–71. Justice Frankfurter's letter to Judge Hand is quoted in Hirsch, cited above, p. 182. The inherited dispute between the law clerks is reported in Simon, *Independent Journey: The Life of William O. Douglas* (1980), p. 218.

CHAPTER VI

The decision of the District Court in the Ballard case is reported at 35 F. Supp. 105 (S.D.Cal. 1940), of the Court of Appeals at 138 F.2d 540 (9th Cir. 1943), of the Supreme Court at 322 U.S. 78 (1944). The quotation from Justice Douglas' opinion is at 86–87, from Justice Jackson's dissent at 92–95. The Ballards were convicted but their conviction was ultimately reversed because women had been systematically excluded from the jury. 329 U.S. 187 (1946).

Ex Parte Thomas, 141 Tex. 591, 174 S.W.2d 958 (1943), reversed under the name Thomas v. Collins, 323 U.S. 516 (1945).

Girouard v. United States, 328 U.S. 61 (1946). The quotation from Justice Douglas' opinion is at 66.

United States v. Schwimmer, 279 U.S. 644 (1929). Justice Holmes' dissenting opinion is at 653–54. For the aftermath of the Schwimmer case see Chief Justice Stone's dissenting opinion in Girouard at 70–79.

For conscription cases decided prior to the Court's decision in Girouard see Arver v. United States, 245 U.S. 366 (1918) and Hamilton v. Regents of California, 293 U.S. 245 (1934). The Court reiterated its holding that the free exercise clause does not require the exemption from military service of religious conscientious objectors, and that the establishment clause does not preclude their exemption, in United States v. Seeger, 380 U.S. 246 (1965), Welsh v. United States, 398 U.S. 408 (1970), and Gillette v. United States, 401 U.S. 437 (1971).

CHAPTER VII

Everson v. Board of Education of Ewing Township, 330 U.S. 1 (1947). The quotations from Justice Black's opinion are at 15, Justice Jackson's Byron quotation is at 19. Justice Rutledge's dissenting opinion is at 28 et seq.

The self-incrimination case decided by the Court shortly after Everson was Adamson v. California, 332 U.S. 46 (1947). The quotations from Justice Frankfurter's opinion are at 62–66. The quotation from Frankfurter's friend is taken from Hirsch, *The Enigma of Felix Frankfurter* (1981), p. 179.

The quotation from Father Murray is from his article, "Law or Prepossessions," 14 Law and Contemp. Probs. 23, 33 (1949).

Fairman, "Does the Fourteenth Amendment Incorporate the Bill of Rights? The Original Understanding," 2 Stanford Law Review 5, 139 (1949).

Morrison, "Does the Fourteenth Amendment Incorporate the Bill of Rights? The Judicial Interpretation," 2 Stanford Law Review 140, 161 (1949).

For an excellent, comprehensive discussion of the incorporation doctrine, see Berger, *Government by Judiciary: The Transformation of the Fourteenth Amendment* (1977), especially Chapter 8: "Incorporation of the Bill of Rights in the Fourteenth Amendment."

CHAPTER VIII

The Bible quotations are from *The New English Bible* (Oxford U. Press, 1976).

McCollum v. Board of Education, 333 U.S. 203 (1948). The quotation from Justice Black's opinion is at 209–10. Justice Frankfurter's concurring opinion is at 212–32. The personal background of the McCollum case is taken largely from Vashti McCollum, *One Woman's Fight* (rev. ed., 1961). The quotation from her father's book, of which the Library of Congress has never heard (perhaps it was printed privately), is taken from her book,

p. 15. For the aftermath of the McCollum case see Mrs. McCollum's book cited above and Patric, "The Impact of a Court Decision: Aftermath of the McCollum Case," 6 J. of Public Law 455 (1957).

Cantwell v. Connecticut, 310 U.S. 296 (1940), discussed in Chapter IV.

The Oregon case in which the Supreme Court held that parents have a constitutional right to send their children to private school was Pierce v. Society of the Sisters of the Holy Names of Jesus and Mary, 268 U.S. 510 (1925), discussed in Chapter II.

The second Witness flag salute case was Board of Education v. Barnette, 319 U.S. 624 (1943), discussed in Chapter V.

The amplified Witness case was Saia v. New York, 334 U.S. 558 (1948). The quotation from Justice Douglas' opinion is at 561. The quotations from Justice Jackson's dissent are at 567 and 569–70, respectively.

The "leading constitutional scholar" was Edward Corwin, Professor Emeritus of Jurisprudence at Princeton University. The quotation is from his article, "The Supreme Court as National School Board," 14 Law and Contemp. Probs. 3, 8 (1949).

CHAPTER IX

Kunz v. People of the State of New York, 340 U.S. 290 (1951). The quotation from the Court's opinion is at 295. Justice Jackson's dissent is at 295–314. The "fighting words" doctrine was enunciated by the Supreme Court in Chaplinsky v. New Hampshire, 315 U.S. 568 (1942).

The New York released time case was Zorach v. Clauson, 343 U.S. 306 (1952). The famous Douglas quotation is at 313. The quotation from Justice Jackson's opinion is at 325.

The Maryland blue law case was McGowan v. State of Maryland, 366 U.S. 420 (1961). The quotation from the Maryland Supreme Court is from Kilgour v. Miles, 6 Gill & J. 268, 274 (1834). The Massachusetts blue law was under attack in two cases, Braunfeld v. Brown, 366 U.S. 599 (1961) and Gallagher v. Crown Kosher Super Market, 366 U.S. 458 (1961). The quotation from Chief Justice Warren's opinion referring to the "inconvenience" of the law is at 605, his solicitude for Sunday Sabbatarians at 609. The quotation from Justice Brennan's dissent is at 611, from Justice Stewart's dissent at 616. Justice Douglas' dissenting opinion is at 561–81.

CHAPTER X

The Regents' Prayer case was Engel v. Vitale. The trial judge's decision is reported at 191 N.Y.Supp.2d 453 (Sup.Ct., Nassau Co., 1959), the Appellate Division decision at 11 A.D.2d 340, 206 N.Y.Supp.2d 183 (2d Dept., 1960), the Court of Appeals decision at 10 N.Y.2d 174, 218 N.Y.Supp.2d 659, 176 N.E.2d 579 (1961), the Supreme Court decision at 370 U.S. 421 (1962).

Bishop Pike is quoted in Katz, *Religion and American Constitutions* (1964), p. 35, Cardinal Spellman is quoted at p. 36. Father Drinan's response is taken from his book, *Religion, The Courts and Public Policy* (1963), p. 120. Former Presidents Hoover and Eisenhower, the Episcopal clergymen in congress assembled, and the Los Angeles municipal judge are quoted in Time, July 6, 1962, p. 8. The resolution of the Governors' Conference is reported in Hachten (the "professor of journalism"), "Journalism and the Prayer Decision," Columbia Journalism Review (Fall 1962), p. 7. Leo Pfeffer is quoted in Rice, *The Supreme Court and Public Prayer* (1964), p. 5.

The Whitestone, New York case is Stein v. Oshinsky. The District Court's decision is reported at 224 F. Supp. 757 (E.D.N.Y. 1963), the Court of Appeals' at 348 F.2d 999 (2d Cir. 1965). The ironic quotation is at 1002. The Supreme Court declined to hear an appeal at 382 U.S. 957 (1965). See also DeSpain v. DeKalb County Community School District, 384 F.2d 836 (7th Cir. 1967), *cert. denied,* 88 S.Ct. 815 (1968).

CHAPTER XI

The background material on the Murray case comes from William J. Murray, *My Life Without God* (1982).

The Pennsylvania and Baltimore Bible-reading cases were decided together in School District of Abington Township v. Schempp, 374 U.S. 203 (1963). The quotation from Justice Brennan's opinion is at 232. Bishop Pike is quoted in Time, June 28, 1963, p. 14. The Wall Street Journal editorial is in its issue of June 19, 1963, p. 12. See also, McGraw, "Secular Humanism and the Schools: The Issue Whose Time Has Come (Heritage Foundation, 1976).

CHAPTER XII

The amended New York education law was Chapter 320, Section 1 of New York Session Laws 1965, compiled as N.Y. Educ. Law, Sec. 701

(1967 Supp.). It was upheld in Board of Education v. Allen, 392 U.S. 236 (1968). The Louisiana precedent was Cochran v. State Board of Education, 281 U.S. 370 (1930).

The Arkansas anti-evolution case was Epperson v. Arkansas. The decision of the Arkansas Supreme Court is reported at 242 Ark. 922, 416 S.W.2d 322 (1967), of the United States Supreme Court at 393 U.S. 97 (1968). The quotation from Justice Harlan's opinion is at 114–15. The famous "monkey trial" case was Scopes v. State, 154 Tenn. 105, 289 S.W. 363 (1927). Vagueness was held to invalidate a criminal statute in Lanzetta v. New Jersey, 306 U.S. 451 (1939)

Walz v. Tax Commission of the City of New York, 397 U.S. 664 (1970). Justice Douglas' dissenting opinion is at 700–16, the Chief Justice's conclusion at 678.

CHAPTER XIII

The Rhode Island and Pennsylvania school subsidy statutes were decided together in Lemon v. Kurtzman, 403 U.S. 602 (1971). Chief Justice Burger's famous (or infamous) tripartite establishment clause test is set forth at 612–13, his conclusion at 614. The quotation from Justice White's dissent is at 668.

The federal Higher Education Facilities Act was upheld in Tilton v. Richardson, 403 U.S. 672 (1971).

The Amish school-leaving case was Wisconsin v. Yoder, 406 U.S. 205 (1972). The quotation regarding medieval religious orders is at 223.

Compulsory chapel at the national military academies was held unconstitutional in Anderson v. Laird, 466 F.2d 283 (D.C. Cir.), *cert. denied*, 409 U.S. 1076 (1972).

The first New York textbook-loan statute was upheld in Board of Education v. Allen, 392 U.S. 236 (1968), discussed in Chapter XI. The new expanded statute was struck down in Committee for Public Education and Religious Liberty v. Nyquist, 413 U.S. 756 (1973). The quotation from the Court's opinion is at 788.

The New York statute providing reimbursement to private schools for the costs of administering state-mandated examinations was struck down in Levitt v. Committee for Public Education and Religious Liberty, 413 U.S. 472 (1973). The quotation from Chief Justice Burger's opinion is at 480.

The Pennsylvania statute furnishing certain books, materials, and secular services to private schools was decimated in Meek v. Pettinger, 421 U.S. 349 (1975). The quotation from Chief Justice Burger's opinion is at 386–87, from Justice Rehnquist's at 395.

The Maryland private college assistance statute was upheld in Roemer v. Board of Public Works of Maryland, 426 U.S. 736 (1976).

The New Hampshire license plate case was Wooley v. Maynard, 430 U.S. 705 (1977). The quotation from Chief Justice Burger's opinion is at 713. ("In God We Trust" on the coinage was upheld in Aranow v. United States, 432 F.2d 242 (9th Cir. 1970), but the Supreme Court has never decided the issue.)

The Ohio case in which a scorecard was needed to decipher the holding was Wolman v. Walter, 433 U.S. 229 (1977).

The Tennessee case in which the constitutional prohibition of clergymen in the legislature was voided was McDaniel v. Paty, 435 U.S. 618 (1978).

NLRB v. Catholic Bishop of Chicago, 440 U.S. 490 (1979).

CHAPTER XIV

New York's revised statute reimbursing private schools for state-mandated examinations was upheld in Committee for Public Education and Religious Liberty v. Regan, 100 S. Ct. 840 (1980).

Florey v. Sioux Falls School District, 619 F.2d 1311 (8th Cir.), *cert. denied,* 449 U.S. 987 (1980).

The Ten Commandments case was Stone v. Graham, 449 U.S. 39 (1980).

Thomas v. Review Board of Indiana Employment Security Division, 450 U.S. 707 (1981).

Heffron v. International Society for Krishna Consciousness, Inc., 452 U.S. 640 (1981).

The Arizona prayer case was Collins v. Chandler Unified School District, 644 F.2d 759 (9th Cir.), *cert. denied,* 102 S.Ct. 322 (1981).

The University of Missouri case was reported as Chess v. Widmar in the District Court at 480 F. Supp. 907 (W.D.Mo. 1979) and in the Court of Appeals at 635 F.2d 1310 (8th Cir. 1980), and as Widmar v. Vincent in the Supreme Court at 454 U.S. 263 (1981).

The Second Circuit prayer case was Brandon v. Bd. of Ed., 635 F.2d 971 (2d Cir. 1980), *cert. denied,* 454 U.S. 1123 (1981), *rehearing denied,*

455 U.S. 983 (1982). The quotation from Judge Kaufman's opinion is at 635 F.2d 978.

The Papal Mass case was O'Hair v. Andrus, 613 F.2d 931 (D.C.Cir. 1979), *cert. denied,* 454 U.S. 263 (1981).

The Jefferson Parish case was Karen B. v. Treen, 653 F.2d 897 (5th Cir. 1981), *aff'd,* 455 U.S. 913 (1982).

CHAPTER XV

Valley Forge Christian College v. Americans United for Separation of Church and State, 454 U.S. 464 (1982). The quotations from Justice Rehnquist's opinion are at 473 and 487, respectively.

The Amish social security tax case was United States v. Lee, 455 U.S. 252 (1982). The quotations from Chief Justice Burger's opinion are at 259 and 261, respectively.

The Grendel's Den case was reported in the District Court as Grendel's Den, Inc. v. Goodwin, 495 F. Supp. 761 (D. Mass. 1980), in the Court of Appeals under the same name at 662 F.2d 88 (1st Cir.) and 662 F.2d 102 (1st Cir. 1981) (en banc), and in the Supreme Court as Larkin v. Grendel's Den, Inc., 103 S. Ct. 505 (1982).

The Jewish basketball players case was Menora v. Illinois High School Association, 683 F.2d 1030 (7th Cir. 1982), *cert. denied,* 51 U.S.L.W. 3533 (1983).

The Minnesota tuition tax-deduction case was Mueller v. Allen, 676 F.2d 1195 (8th Cir. 1982) (quotation at 1198), *aff'd,* 463 U.S. 388 (1983). Milton and Rose Friedman advocate vouchers in, among other places, their iconoclastic book, *Free to Choose* (1980), p. 164. On the issue we are considering they write:

> Indeed, we believe that the penalty that is now imposed on parents who do not send their children to public schools violates the spirit of the First Amendment, whatever lawyers and judges may decide about the letter. Public schools teach religion, too— not a formal, theistic religion, but a set of values and beliefs that constitute a religion in all but name. The present arrangements abridge the religious freedom of parents who do not accept the religion taught by the public schools yet are forced to pay to have their children indoctrinated with it, and to pay still more to have their children escape indoctrination.

The Nebraska legislature prayer case was reported in the District Court as Chambers v. Marsh, 504 F. Supp. 585 (D.Neb. 1980), in the Court of

Appeals under the same name at 675 F.2d 228 (8th Cir. 1982), and in the Supreme Court as Marsh v. Chambers, 463 U.S. 783 (1983).

Virgin Mary on a postage stamp: Protestants and Other Americans United for Separation of Church and State v. O'Brien, 272 F. Supp. 712 (D.D.C. 1967).

Fifty-foot Cross: Meyer v. Oklahoma City, 496 P.2d 789 (Okla. 1972), *cert. denied,* 409 U.S. 980 (1973).

Ten Commandments: Anderson v. Salt Lake City Corp., 475 F.2d 29 (10th Cir. 1973).

Veterans' War Memorial Cross: Eugene Sand & Gravel, Inc. v. City of Eugene, 276 Or. 1007, 558 P.2d 338 (1976).

Los Angeles City Hall as bulletin board: Fox v. City of Los Angeles, 22 Cal.3d 792, 150 Cal. Rptr. 867, 587 P.2d 663 (1978).

Allen v. Morton, 495 F.2d 65 (D.C.Cir. 1973). The Lubavitcher Menorah is reported in Time, December 20, 1982, p. 54.

The Pawtucket crèche case was Donnelly v. Lynch, reported in the District Court at 525 F. Supp. 1150 (D.R.I. 1981), in the Court of Appeals at 691 F.2d 1029 (1st Cir. 1982), and in the Supreme Court at 465 U.S. 668 (1984).

CHAPTER XVI

The New York and Grand Rapids cases involving remedial aid to deprived school children were Aguilar v. Felton, 87 L.Ed.2d 290 (1985) and Grand Rapids School District v. Ball, 87 L.Ed.2d 267 (1985).

The Alabama silent prayer case was Wallace v. Jaffree, 86 L.Ed.2d 29 (1985).

The prayer fellowship case was Bender v. Williamsport Area School District, 741 F.2d 538 (3d Cir. 1984), *rev'd,* 54 U.S.L.W. 4307 (1986).

The case involving an Air Force captain ordered to remove his yarmulke was Goldman v. Weinberger, 54 U.S.L.W. 4298 (1986).

CONCLUSION

As this chapter is based primarily on materials already presented, citations are only to new materials.

Tribe, *American Constitutional Law* (1978), p. 819.

An Indian tribe was permitted to use peyote in People v. Woody, 61 Cal.2d 716, 40 Cal. Rptr. 69, 394 P.2d 813 (1964). A young man in

Chapel Hill, North Carolina was not able to use this precedent to justify his possession of marijuana. State of North Carolina v. Bullard, 267 N.C. 599 (1966).

A federal law disfranchising polygamy-practicing Mormons was upheld in Davis v. Beason, 133 U.S. 333 (1890).

Letters of William M. Leach, Jr., attorney general of Tennessee, to Senator Victor H. Ashe dated March 22, 1982 and February 18, 1983, and to Representative Frank Buck dated March 22, 1982.

Students' rights: to determine their own dress, Bannister v. Paradis, 316 F. Supp. 185 (D.N.H. 1970); to determine their own hairstyles, Bishop v. Colaw, 450 F.2d 1069 (8th Cir. 1971); and to demonstrate on school premises during the school day, Tinker V. Des Moines Indiana Community School District, 393 U.S. 503 (1969).

Jesuit: Costanzo, *This Nation Under God: Church, State and School in America* (1964), p. 131.

H.J. Res. 279 was introduced in the 99th Congress, 1st Session, and was referred to the Committee on the Judiciary, whence it was never heard from again.

Morgan, *Disabling America: The "Rights Industry" in Our Time* (1984), p. 44.

New York Superintendent of Schools: quoted in Engel v. Vitale, 191 N.Y.Supp.2d 453, 460 (Sup. Ct., Nassau Co., 1959).

Leading Religion Cases

Index

(Dates in parentheses refer to periods of service of United States Supreme Court Justices. As the entire book concerns the religion clause of the First Amendment, there are no references here to "First Amendment," "free exercise," or "establishment.")

163